I0020130

JavaScript Programming

A Comprehensive Programming Guide for Beginners That Will Enable You to Improve JavaScript Skills

By: Ethem Mining

2

Disclaimer Notice.

Please note the information contained within this document is for educational and entertainment purposes only. This book not intended to be a substitute for medical advice. Please consult your health care provider for medical advice and treatment.

Table Of Contents

Introduction

Chapter 1: What is JavaScript?

Chapter 2: JavaScript Variables

Chapter 3: Operators in JavaScript

Chapter 4: JavaScript functions

Chapter 5: JavaScript Objects

Chapter 6: Document Object Model

Chapter 7: JavaScript Cookies

Chapter 8: Regular Expression

Chapter 9: HTML5 APIS

Conclusion

Introduction

JavaScript in the complex world of technology is referred to basically as the programming language used by the World Wide Web (the internet) that is commonly written as www. This book is a perfect guide and study book as it delves deeper into this programming language arming you with all you will need to know about JavaScript as a language. Programming by definition can basically be described as the act of building programs (in this case coding) designed with the sole purpose of directing a computer in what acts to perform to achieve a certain goal, it as well describes specifically how these acts are to be undertaken and the exact time these acts are to be performed in order to give results that are expected. Today in the world of science and technology, it can be said a large percentage of all websites available online use JavaScript as is all web browsers used on all devices including desktops, tablets and smartphones as well as laptops and gaming devices. This is a remarkable change in the world of technology as different devices have different capabilities and yet JavaScript is the common thing that runs in them. This is basically the new age of computer technology armed with more improvements that ensure your devices perform even better and faster as well making sure you accomplish your desired tasks more efficiently and enjoy it too.

A programming language is generally defined as an advanced language that is basically designed with the specified purpose of directing, commanding and manipulating computers in order to attain a number of goals that have been set. JavaScript is said to be the most effective way of communicating with a computer and simply the computer can gain knowledge and to some extend store knowledge and be able to run on itself without the help of human intervention. This is possible when a computer has been programmed to carry on with different or specific tasks without the need for human supervision. There is a great similarity in how both humans and computers communicate. For one the languages used by humans and computers both have the provision of utilizing certain wordings and phrasings that are fused differently in ways they haven't before, bringing life to new approaches in how computers are used.

It is then safe to say that a programmer is a person that is well equipped with the knowledge of programming and hence designs a program for a computer as per their wish and particular need. A program is therefore fundamental in how you use a computer and without it you cannot be able to accomplish anything. It is the link between the idea that the programmer has and the final results that they want to achieve. It helps the computer perform its various tasks, know how and where to store information as well.

Chapter 1: What is JavaScript?

JavaScript is what is fondly referred to as a lightweight, and is widely used and most easily accessible computer programming language ever created to date with access guaranteed all across the world. Basically JavaScript performs in HTML pages by enabling users to associate with Client-side Script resulting in pages that are said to be new age as well as interactive. JavaScript as a program was created and meant for creating a network-centric software that enables their user(s) to attain certain set goals at a given timeline. JavaScript is said to be a program that is not hard to use and can be used using any browser available to the user provided the user knows the basics of running a program and using a computer as well.

1.1 History of JavaScript

In 1995, the most widely used and available browser was from Netscape which had its numerous limitations one being its accesability. With more and more content being intended for webpages, there was a need to design a new program that enabled content added to these pages to be more appealing and interactive. This resulted in the creation of JavaScript by Brendan Eich. As a result of its rather revolutionary changes to how webpages are designed, all the browsers available today use JavaScript and there are standards that are set to ensure that their creating companies adhere to the set JavaScript guidelines.

JavaScript however should in no way ever be compared to the older programming language Java.

The names are simply similar because the marketers of JavaScript saw the name as better for marketing purposes other than coming up with a whole new name and making people know it afresh. Therefore it is essential for JavaScript users to know this information and not get the two confused.

At the time of coming up with JavaScript, Java already had a great following due to extensive marketing campaigns as they go to a program and was gaining popularity with every new user. It then became simpler to come up with a name that could be associated with Java and this made all the difference resulting in JavaScript widespread popularity to date.

When JavaScript became available to other up and coming browsers other than Netscape, there arose a need to come up with a set of rules that every user had to adhere to while using the programming language. This ensured every browser that advertised to be using JavaScript was truthful and not cutting corners. The document was named the ECMA Script. It was written by the ECMA (European Computer Manufacturers Association) which the organization is charged with the mandate to come up with the guidelines in the first place. It is important to note that there is no difference between JavaScript and ECMA-Script; it is just different names used to mean the very same thing.

There have been several versions of JavaScript that have been written since the initial version was released.

It was between the years 2000 and 2010 that JavaScript rose in popularity and global domination. The version that was available at this time was JavaScript version 3. At the same time programmers were in the midst of designing version 4 which had promised to be more revolutionary at its best. However it never saw the light of day. To save face from this failure, they came up with JavaScript version 5 in 2009 which never met expectations at all only making a few improvements at best. Later in 2015, version 6 was released and in some ways was able to accomplish some of the initial targets that had been set for version 4 which had not been touched until now. There are improvements being released annually as well.

Of importance to take not of is that it is not browsers which are the sole platforms that can make use of JavaScript.Other databases for example the Mongo DB requires JavaScript as their coding and questions language method.

Due to the inevitability to change, browsers have to constantly keep up with the evolution of the programming language by being up to date with every new version released and the changes that come with it.

Old browsers may not support every feature the language provides therefore users will be forced to purchase newer versions if they wish to utilize the new improvements they come with. It is always worth noting that JavaScript programmers are always striving to keep the basics the same and not in any large way alter the initial as well as already created designs which means that the latest browsers in use can still be able to support the older versions but with certain limitations.

1.2 Benefits of using JavaScript

A major point to note is the Client-side JavaScript is known as the one programming language that is used the most by very many users worldwide. It is therefore a must for it to be part of any HTML document if user(s) will have their written code recognized by the browser they are using.

Therefore JavaScript is known to provide a wide array of benefits as compared to other programs that may be used in place of it. A benefit of JavaScript is the ability to note if a user has keyed in the right email address as needed. If not, then a correction will be made immediately. Another benefit is JavaScript can be utilized to initiate some moments including clicking of certain buttons, navigation link plus other similar actions as per the user(s) needs.

1.3 What does JavaScript do?

As earlier noted, JavaScript ranks as the top most used language of programming as is utilized by every browser version available today. It is therefore important to know what JavaScript does. Below are a few details of what is does:

- JavaScript is designed in a way that its users are always able to be in charge of their browsers.

- JavaScript is able to identify the specific browser being used by the user plus the Operating system as well. This enables it to function as per the functions being performed.

- JavaScript is equipped with a calculator that enables users to work out some problems.

- JavaScript is able to warn a user when an invalid input has been made immediately and be able to correct it as needed.

- A JavaScript user can always be able to come up with new functions that are contained in scripts.

JavaScript also possess some limitations and they are as follows:

- For one JavaScript lacks multithreading capabilities which means it cannot be able to execute a number of multithreads at the same time.

- JavaScript is not designed in a way that it can be able to gain access to pages that are on other domains.

- There are some databases that JavaScript is not able to access without there being a server side script. However it is worth noting that there are some client side ones that a user can obtain.

- A user of JavaScript is not permitted to write a file that is on the server side without use of an Ajax request which will in turn do this.

- There is a limitation on how many devices a user is able to use with JavaScript.

- Different browsers interpret JavaScript differently which results in very different outputs.

1.4 Environment Setup

A great characteristic of JavaScript is its minimal and not very expensive requirements needed to get started in using it. A user can be content with starting with what they have in hand in terms of a writing pad. A compiler is deemed unnecessary at first because JavaScript is simply translated by the browser being used.

1.5 JavaScript Editing Tools

There are simpler to use JavaScript editing tools and they include:

- Brackets
- Visual studio code
- Atom
- Neovim
- Sublime text
- Vim
- Emacs
- Komodo
- TextMate

1.6 JavaScript Example

<script> tags are usually used to contain our JavaScript statements. The script tag can be placed anywhere on your webpage as required. It is important to remember to always maintain it inside the <head> so as to achieve the right outcome.

An example that can be used to first illustrate this is one that can help print out "Hello World". So as to ensure our code remains even when using a browser that isn't able to use JavaScript, it is important to feed a JavaScript code inside of an HTML code. Observe the code below:

```
<html>

<body>

<script language="JavaScript" type="text/java script">

<!--
          document. Write ("Hello World!")
//-->
</script>

</body>

</html>
```

The result that will be achieved from the above code is:

Hello World!

Here '//' is symbolic of a phrase that is found in JavaScript that is added to block any browser from translating the last HTML phrase like a JavaScript code portion.

Chapter 2: JavaScript Variables

The storage area where designed programs have the ability to change and utilize stored data is what is known as JavaScript variable. JavaScript has such variables in it. Variables can be imagined as named containers that hold the storage location of value. Data can be placed into these containers following this with a way to distinguish one container from the next which is by naming them differently.

Variables must be declared first before they are put into any use in our programs. By use of the keyword var, we are able to declare variables in our program. An example of declaring a variable is as shown in the illustration below:

```
<script type="text/javascript">
var number;
var price;
</script>
```

Variable declaration.

Declaration of variable simply means it is charged with the mandate to show credible proof of there being a variable of a specific form as well as name enabling the browser to move forward with translation without the need of the full 53variable.

Initializing a variable.

Initializing a variable is said to be the ability to store a value within a said variable. This can be performed at a time when the variable is being created or much later when a user will require said variable.

An example to illustrate this is as follows. Create a variable named **sign** and let it have the value 16. Another variable will be named **date** and will be initialized to **Sophia**

```
/<script type="text/javascript">
var name="Sophia";
var sign;
age= 16;
```

The main word var is used only to initialize only once in any lifetime of a variable name within the coding. Note that the variable should not be declared twice.

It is common within JavaScript to observe a variable holding a value and it can be in any type of data it needs to be in. JavaScript is different from other languages available in that during announcing, it is not a must you inform it the form of value the said variable will contain in it.

2.1 JavaScript Variable Scope

JavaScript scope can be said to be the code that is available at the present moment that will in turn determine how JavaScript will be able to reach variables. This is achieved used only two scopes in JavaScript.

They are:

- A variable that is global in nature: This is the type of variable that is worldwide and can therefore be translated at any place within JavaScript code.

- A variable that is local in nature: This is the type of variable that is locally visible and solely via a function.

It is important to note that local variables are more popular than global variables even with name similarity inside of a function. An example is when you decide to establish a local variable like variable count which is similarly named as the global variable, the local variable will be seen and the global one hidden as a result.

A simple example below shows the difference in the visibility of a local variable against:

```javascript
<script type="text/javascript">
var count=10; //Declare a global variable
function takeCount(   ) {

            var count=20; //Declare a local variable
        while(count<30     ){
                ++count;
}         document.write( count   );
}
</script>
```

The output result is as follows:

21

22

23

24

25

26

27

28

29

2.2 Types of JavaScript data

Types of JavaScript data can be described simply as the method by which both variables and functions are to be declared. This is done by having the type of function or variable be the determinant of the volume of space needed by it in storage resulting in its bit pattern translation as well. In JavaScript, there are three used types of data. They include:

- Strings e.g. " This is JavaScript Tutorial"

- Numbers, e.g. 123, 560.7, etc.

- Boolean, e.g. true or false.

Strings

They are representative of texts and are characterized by being written in between quotes all the time.

'Up in the sky'
'Fly in the sky'
'Float in the sky'

Users are at liberty to make use of any kind of quotes between singular ones, double ones and also use of back ticks as well is permitted when creating strings. What a user needs to remember is to use the same ones always in the text required in order to maintain the setup at hand.

Note that in order to be able to have such formats in a string, a user must follow a certain notation. Always include a backslash \ in between the text that is quoted to indicate it is of special meaning. It is what is known as character escaping. Make sure you remember to have the backslash in between the quote and never at the end of it.

By having an n character appear after the backslash \ a user simply means that they are creating a newline. By having a t character appear after the backslash\ a user simply means that the user is creating a tab character as well. A simple example is as shown below:

'Here is the initial line\n and here is the following line'

Numbers

JavaScript is characterized by its use of a precise number of bits which amount always to 64 in order for it to successfully store a number. This means that there is a limit to the number of patterns a user is able to come up with using 64 bits resulting in a limit as well in the numbers to be availed. An example is with X decimal digits, a user can only avail 10X numbers. This means that if a user has only 64 binary characters, they will only avail of 264 numbers.

It is worth noting that a while back there was a limit to the amount of storage that a computer had resulting in users only being limited to groups that were in between 8 and 16 bits to avail their numbers. This means they had to be extra careful so as not to lead to overflow such numbers resulting in a number that is too big for the bit needed. The same cannot be said about the amount of storage in devices as devices like smart phones that are much smaller have ample memory in them. This gives the user freedom to explore 64 bit numbers that are much bigger only being careful when handling numbers that are even much, much bigger and can easily overflow then. Those that are not extremely big are safer.

Boolean

An important point for a user to note is the value of having a character that is used to indicate the difference between essentially two outcomes only. This can either be 'right' and 'left' or 'up' and 'down' as well. JavaScript therefore has what is called a Boolean type which is characterized by only two outcomes that are 'true' and 'false'.

Another point to note is the ability of JavaScript to translate two types of trivial data that is undefined and null, having both of them translate one value only at any given time.

It is important for a user to note that in JavaScript, it is common for all numbers to be displayed as values that are said to be floating-point. The IEEE 754 set the standard that JavaScript display numbers by making use of the 64-bit format of floating-point.

2.3 Types of JavaScript Comments

In JavaScript, it is the comments C and C++ that are mainly used. These comments used in JavaScript can be represented as follows:

- Text that appears in the middle of the \\ sign at the line's ending considering it being a comment resulting in JavaScript ignoring it.

- Test that appears in between /* and */ is too a comment and will result in multiple lines.

- <!—is an HTML sequence that opens comment which is accepted by JavaScript and is interpreted as a comment that is a single line similar to //comment.

```
<script language="javascript"  type="text/javascript">
<!- -

//This is a comment. It is similar to comments in  c++
/*

  *This is a multline comment in JavaScript

   * It is very similar to comments in C programming
*/

//- ->

</script>
```

Chapter 3: Operators in JavaScript

In JavaScript, an operator is defined as a representation charged with the mandate of instructing the compiler to undertake certain computations with the end result being the targeted result. JavaScript can be able to handle a variety of these operators and they include:

- The Operators of Arithmetic

- The Operators of Comparison

- The Operators of logical/ relational

- The Operators of assignment

- The Operators of conditional/ ternary

3.1 Arithmetic Operators

JavaScript does support arithmetic operators. These arithmetic operators include:

For Example let's assume we have 2 variables that are A and B and each variable holds data value 10 and 20 respectively, then:

Operator and description
+ , that Adds variable A and B to give 30
- , that subtracts B from A and gives a negative 10
* , that multiplies both A and B and gives 200
/ , that Divides B by A and gives 2
% , that puts the remaining of a division of an integer to result in 0
++ , tops up by one the integer
-- , that Decreases integer value by 1 to vive 9

The Additional operator does work numerically as well as string data types. Below is a program that shows types of arithmetic operation in JavaScript:

```
<html>
<head>

</head>

<body>

<script type="text/javascript">

var a=33;

var b=10;

var c="String";

var linebreak="<br/>";

document.write("a+b= " );

result= a+b;

document.write( result);

document.write(linebreak);

document.write( "a -b= " );

result= a-b;

document.write(result);

document.write( linebreak );

document.write( "a/b=" );

result=a/b ;

document.write(result) ;

document.write(linebreak);
```

```
document.write("a % b = ");

result = a % b;
document.write(result);
document.write(linebreak);



document.write("a + b + c = ");
result = a + b + c;
document.write(result);
document.write(linebreak);



a = a++;
document.write("a++ = ");
result = a++;
document.write(result);
document.write(linebreak);




b = b--;
document.write("b-- = ");
result = b--;
document.write(result);
document.write(linebreak);

</script>

</body>
```

The reached result of the output is as below:

```
a + b = 43

a - b = 23

a / b = 3.3

a % b = 3

a + b + c = 43Test
```

3.2 Comparison Operators

The strings ordered are roughly alphabetic and not the expected in a dictionary which dictates that uppercase letters have "less" than the opposite ones, so "Z" < "a", and no alphabetic characters (!, -, and so on) are within in the ordering. When we compare strings, JavaScript goes beyond the order of characters given from left to right, comparing Unicode codes one by one systematically. Similar operators are >= (greater than or equal to), <= (less than or equal to), == (equal to), and !(not equal to).

```
console.log("Itchy" != "Scratchy")
// → true
console.log("Apple =="Orange" )
//→ false
```

It is vital to note that only one value in JavaScript is not equal to itself, the NaN ("not a number).

The following comparison operators are supported by JavaScript:

For example let us assume we have two variables that are said A and B and each variable holds data value 10 and 20 respectively, then:

Operator	Description
== (Equal)	Checks if the values are equal or not, if yes, then the state is true. Ex: (A==B) is not true
!=(Equal)	Checks if the values are equal or not, if not, then the state becomes true. Ex: (A!=B) is not true
>(Greater than)	Checks if the value of the left digit is greater than value of the right, if yes, then the condition is true. Ex: (A>B) is true
< (Less than)	Checks if the value of the left operand is less than value of the right, if it is, then the state becomes true. Ex: (A<B) is true
>= (Greater than or Equal to)	inquires if the value of left operand is greater than or equal to value of the right, if it's the same, then the condition is true. Ex: (A> =B) is not true
<=(Less than or Equal to)	Checks if the left operand value is less than or equal to value of the right, if yes, then the condition is considered true. Ex: (A<=B) is not true

The code below illustrates the usage of comparison operators in JavaScript coding.

```html
<html>
<body>
<script type="text/javascript">
var a = 10;
var b = 20;
var linebreak = "<br />";
document.write("(a == b) => ");
result = (a == b);
document.write(result);
document.write(linebreak);
document.write("(a < b) => ");
result = (a < b);
document.write(result);
document.write(linebreak);
document.write("(a > b) => ");
```

The resulting output is as follows:

```
(a == b) => false

(a < b) => true

(a > b) => false

(a != b) => true

(a >= b) => false

(a <= b) => true
```

3.3 Operators that are logical

In JavaScript, only three operators described as logical that are normally supported and they include not, or, and.

It is important to note that logical and is symbolized by && operator resulting in a positive outcome only when the numbers assigned to it are positive as well.

```
console.log (true && false)
// → false
console.log (true && true)
// → true
```

The || operator denotes logical or. It produces true if either of the values given to it is true.

```
console.log (false || true)
// → true

console.log (false || false)
// → false
```

Not is written as an exclamation mark (!). It's a unary operator that flips the value given to it -! true produces false, and !false gives true.

Examples of the operators that are logical and JavaScript support are as follows. (Consider the possibility of Variable X holding 5 and Variable Y holding 10):

Operator	Description
AND Logical (&&)	The two operators for example do not have zero resulting in a positive outcome example of which is X&&Y which is positive.
OR Logical (||)	The two operators as an example do not have zero resulting in a positive outcome of which X||Y is positive.

Below is a sample of JavaScript that makes use of operators that are logical in it:

```html
<html>

<body>

<script type="text/javascript">

<!--
var a = true;

var b = false;

var linebreak = "<br />";

document.write("(a && b) => ");

result = (a && b);

document.write(result);

document.write(linebreak);

document.write("(a || b) => ");

result = (a || b);

document.write(result);

document.write(linebreak);

document.write("!(a && b) => ");

result = (!(a && b));

document.write(result);

document.write(linebreak);

//-->

</script>

</body>

</html>
```

3.4 JavaScript IF-ELSE statements

JavaScript is a program that is best described as one built using both statements and expressions as well. An expression is best defined as a portion of code which results in a value. An expression therefore is all the values that are noted down. It is important to note that it is a common occurrence for expressions to have other expressions amidst them in a similar manner to sentences and sub-sentences too. This intricate format is what is known as nesting which makes it possible for a user to construct expressions that are mathematically complex.

Statements in JavaScript will be able to be in contact with sentences that are full when an expression is also in contact with a portion of a sentence as well. An example of a simple statement is !;

Always take note in every chance that the one using it is permitted by JavaScript to not include the semicolon when ending the statement. Also note that this may not be allowed in certain instances which will need separating of statements.

Expressions at times just output values only to be utilized by codes that are enclosing.

Statements are described as stand-alone in nature and can only be part of a larger role only if its effects are felt globally. On an interface, its appearance can amount to global change.

Some instances arise that require the utilization of only one path out of a number of them. For such instances a user has to apply statements that are conditional and permit their program to produce positive outcomes and act right as well. Below a user will be able to delve deeper into the if-else statement:

There are certain situations that require the need to adopt one out of the usual set of paths.

In this type of situation we require to utilize the information on a conditioned format that allows your program to make the right choices which result in the act that is correct.

Here we shall explain the if-else statement in more depth.

3.4a The if-else flowchart

There are a number of if-else statements that are said to be supported by JavaScript. They include:

- If statement
- If-else statement
- If else if statement

In the flow chart below, a user will get to know how exactly the statement if-else operates.

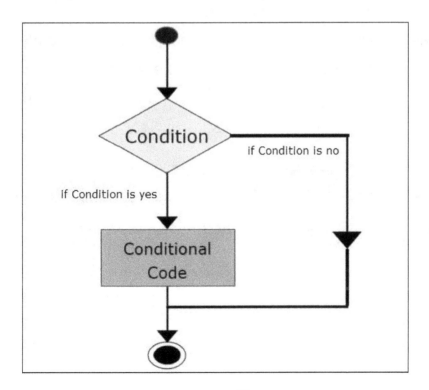

3.4b Statement if

This statement enables JavaScript to be in charge of decision making resulting in absolute execution of statements. It makes use of the following syntax:

If (expression){

Statements to be performed on the off chance the expression is correct }

The expression is processed giving in a real value outcome which means the other statements are processed as well. A false expression will mean no expression will be processed. Decision making is mainly done by comparison operators. The example below shows a variable called age with a data value that is assigned to the variable being 30.

(It is important to note that there is a requirement in the statement if for the expression to have a variable that is above 18 so as to have the statements processed.)

```html
<html>

<body>

<script type= "text/javascript">

var age = 30;

if(age > 18) {

document.write ("<b> Qualifies for an identification card" );

}

</script>

</body>

</html>
```

The output result is:

Qualifies for an identification card

3.4c The statement if-else

This kind of statement permits JavaScript to process statements in a manner that is more contained. The statement if-else has a syntax that is shown below:

```
If ( expression) {
        Statements to be executed if expression is true
}else {
        Statements to be executed if expression is false
}
```

After processing the expression which produces a true outcome, the statements contained in the 'if' group is performed. A false expression means the statements in the 'else' group are the ones to be performed. Below is a sample showing how if-else statement in JavaScript operates:

```
<html>

<body>

<script type= "text/javascript">

var age =15;

if ( age >  18 ) {

          document. write ( "qualifies for driving");

}else {

          document. write ( "no qualifies for driving") ;

}
```

The output result is as follows: *No qualifies for driving*

3.4d The if-else-if statement

In JavaScript, this statement is described as more complex in nature that the if-else statement. This is because of its ability to permit Java Script to select the right output to use out of several outputs that have been given. Below is the syntax used to show this:

```
if( expression 1) {
        Statements to  be executed if expression 1 is true
}else if ( expression 2 ){
        Statements to be executed if the expression 2 is true
}else if ( expression 3) {
        Statements to be executed if the expression  3 is true
} else if ( expression 4) {
        Statements to be executed if the expression  4 is true
}else{
        Statements to  be  executed if no expression is true
}
```

In the above example, there are a number of statements of "if" in which every "if" is a portion of the clause "else" which is from the past statement.

Therefore it is important to note that all statements are conducted according to the nature of their condition whether true or false. In the case of false, the "else" is restricted. Below is an example showing the if-else-if statement being utilized in JavaScript.

```
<html>
<body>
<script type="text/javascript">
<!--
var book = "maths";
if( book == "history" ){
document.write("<b>History Book</b>");
}else if( book == "maths" ){
document.write("<b>Maths Book</b>");
}else if( book == "economics" ){
document.write("<b>Economics Book</b>");
}else{
document.write("<b>Unknown Book</b>");
}
//-->
</script>
</body>
</html>
```

The resulting output is as follows:

Maths Book

3.5 Bindings

Think for example how a program is able to store a state within it. Think also how the same program is able to recall information too. Above the user learnt how new values are essentially made from old ones without tampering with the old ones. Also the user has learnt the importance of utilizing the new values at once or they will disappear. In order to ensure new values are retained, JavaScript utilizes what is known as Binding.

let caught = 6 * 6;

This is the following statement with a keyword that shows that this statement is the one that symbolizes binding. Follow this with the name given to binding and decide whether to give it a value there and then, by=expression & operator.

The user has created a statement known as caught which it then uses to catch the value that is output by the multiplication of 6by6. An expression can then use the name of the binding after it has been caught.

Such an expression has a value that is the same as the one of the caught binding.

An example is as below:

```
let ten = 10;

console.log(ten * ten);

// → 1
```

It is important to note that just because of binding points to a value, it is in no way attached to said value always. The = can be used at any point on the bindings that exist to detach them from the values they have at present and direct them to point at fresh ones.

```
Let mood= "light";
console.log(mood);
//→light
mood="dark";
console.log(mood);
```

Picture bindings always as an arm attached to a larger body. Bindings are not allowed to have values so they get them by catching them. Two bindings are able to make the same value. It is vital to note that any program will only be allowed to use the values that it is associated with. In case the user requires to recall important information, they will simply catch it and hold it in place. An example can also be as follows. To keep in mind the amount of money owed to Carlos, he will create a binding. When he is paid back let say $20, this binding will be awarded a new value which will be minus the $20 which has been paid.


```
let carlosDebt = 100;
carlosDebt = carlosDebt - 20;
console.log(carlosDebt);
// → 80
```

3.6 Binding Names

These names can be any name that is chosen. There is no limit. These names can include numbers as well like true10 which is an accepted name. The only disclaimer here is the number should never come before the letters. Signs and characters which include $ and _ can be used but only those two.

There are words that have a special purpose like let (they are keywords) and cannot be permitted to be used as binging names. Some words have been saved up for use by versions of JavaScript that are yet to be designed and can therefore not be used as binding names as well. These words are very many. Below are some of them :

Enum, public, while, return, default, case, break, delete, switch, function, catch, do, if, package, this, throw, private, implements, else, class, const, export, import, protected, try, debugger, extends, interface, type, false, in, return, of, yield, let, for, with, instance, finally, void, while etc.

3.7 JavaScript Switch-Case

The JavaScript Switch-case statement is the best solution when dealing with a multi-way branch. In the previous sub-chapter we used if...else. If statements in working on the multiway branches. However, it is important to note that the above is not recommended as the perfect method to utilize. This is true primarily when the total number of branches is based on the content of one variable. In version 1.2 of JavaScript a user can utilize a switch statement that is made solely for this purpose with better results than when the user works with if-else-if.

Below is a flow chart showing the statement switch-case:

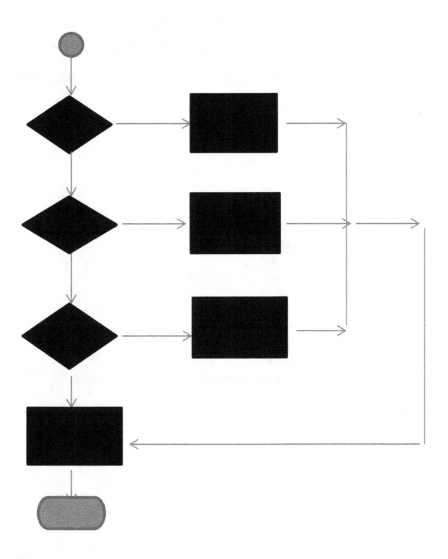

Every user knows the use of the statement switch which is to place the expression to the ability to administer and process them just after the expression value in use.

It is the work of the interpreter to asses every case in accordance with the expression value up to when a similar result will be attained. In an instance where a similar result is not attained, an assigned on will be used.

Below is syntax indicative of this:

```
switch □expression)

{

case condition 1: statement(s)

break;

case condition 2: statement(s)

break;
...
case condition n: statement(s)

break;

default: statement(s)

}
```

A case is brought to a close by a break statement which is indicative of this. A continuation in processing the statements is done when there is a lack of a break statement.

```
<html>

<body>

<script type="text/javascript">
<!--
var grade='A';
```

```
document.write("Entering switch block<br />");

switch (grade)

{

case 'A': document.write("Good job<br />");

case 'B': document.write("Pretty good<br />");

case 'C': document.write("Passed<br />");

case 'D': document.write("Not so good<br />");

case 'F': document.write("Failed<br />");

default: document.write("Unknown grade<br />")

}
document.write("Exiting switch block");

//-->
</script>

</body>

</html>
```

The resulting output is as follows:

```
Entering switch block
Good job
Exiting switch block
```

3.8 JavaScript While Loop

When a JavaScript user is designing a program, they may come across a certain moment where they will be needed to repeat an act more than once. It is in such moments where the user will have to use a While Loop which in turn cuts down the number of lines which the code will have as a result.

Such practices are meant to achieve and maintain high quality coding as well as programming at all times. The purpose of the While Loop which would be discussed in this chapter will be to process blocks of codes or statements over and over again in the presence of a true statement only. In the presence of an expression that is false, the loop will cease at once.

An example of this is illustrated in the chart below:

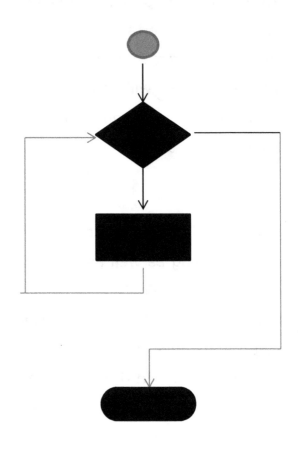

The while loop has made use of the following syntax:

```
while (expression){

Statement(s) to be executed if expression is true

}
```

Below is a sample used to show how a While loop works:

```html
<html>

<body>

<script type="text/javascript">

<!--
var count = 0;

document.write("Starting Loop ");

while (count < 10){

document.write("Current Count : " + count + "<br />");

count++;

}
document.write("Loop stopped!");

//-->
</script>

<p>Set the variable to different value and then try...</p>

</body>

</html>
```

The output is as follows:

```
Starting Loop Current Count : 0

Current Count : 1

Current Count : 2

Current Count : 3

Current Count : 4

Current Count : 5

Current Count : 6
```

3.8a The do While Loop

A loop that is similar to the While Loop with their difference only being the point where the check occurs which is at the point of loop completion rather that at its start. A point to note is that it is a must for a loop to occur multiple times even when faced with a false statement for example. An illustration of this fact is in the chart below:

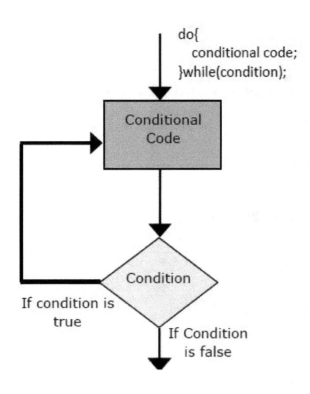

In JavaScript, the syntax indicative of a While Loop is as follows:

```
do{

Statement(s) to be executed;

} while (expression);
```

It is important to always remember that you are not permitted to not include the semicolon placed at the conclusion of the do-while loop so as to achieve a certain goal.

An example that can be used to demonstrate the do-while loop is as shown below:

```html
<html>

<body>

<script type="text/javascript">

<!-

var count = 0;

document.write("Starting Loop" + "<br />");

do{

document.write("Current Count : " + count + "<br />");

count++;

}while (count < 5);

document.write ("Loop stopped!");

//-->

</script>
```

The resulting output of this is as follows:

```
Starting Loop

Current Count : 0

Current Count : 1

Current Count : 2

Current Count : 3

Current Count : 4

Loop Stopped!
```

3.8b For-loop JavaScript

JavaScript makes use of for-loop as well and is said to be made up of three parts. These parts are as follows:

- The Initializing Loop: It is where a user begins their counter with a first number. The beginning statements always come before the commencement of the loop.

- The variable can be assigned any numeric integer as the data value. For example int =0;

- The test statement. It is the one charged with the mandate to check if a certain statement is true or false. In the case of a true statement, the code inside of the loop will be processed accordingly. If it is found to be false, it will cease. For example int i < 20;

- The iterated statement. It is located at the point where the user is able to add or subtract their counter according to the requirement.

It is important to note that all these three parts are separated by semicolons (;).

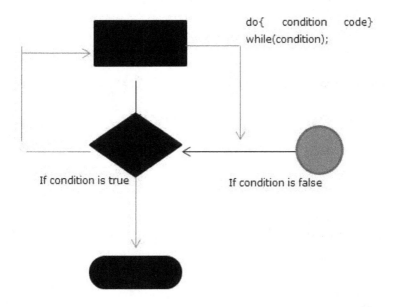

do{   condition   code}
while(condition);

If condition is true   If condition is false

In JavaScript, the syntax to be used here is as follows:

```
for (initialization; test condition; iteration statement){

Statement(s) to be executed if test condition is true
}

<html>

<body>

<script type="text/javascript">

<!--
var count;

document.write("Starting Loop" + "<br />");

for(count = 0; count < 5; count++){

document.write("Current Count : " + count );

document.write("<br />");
```

The resulting result from these is as follows:

```
Starting Loop
Current Count : 0

Current Count : 1

Current Count : 2

Current Count : 3

Current Count : 4
```

In the above example, it is important to note that the variable count is initialized to 0 on the first segment of the for loop and on the second segment there is condition on which the variable should be less than 5, and lastly on the third segment, there exist an increase in the counter of the variable.

3.8c JavaScript For-in-loop

This is the loop in JavaScript charged with the mandate of bringing together objects. This will be clearer in the Object topic to be covered later where the user will get to learn the significance of objects in JavaScript and understand as a result the value of the For-in-loop.

In JavaScript, the for-in-loop syntax is as below:

```
for (variablename in object){
statement or block to execute
}
```

A property removed from an object will be handed a variable name after each loop which happens again and again to completion of all properties available.

The following is a sample indicative of how the for-loop can be used in a JavaScript program.

```
<html>

<body>

<script type="text/javascript">
<!--

var aProperty;

document.write("Navigator Object Properties<br /> ");

for (aProperty in navigator)
{

document.write(aProperty);

document.write("<br />");

}

document.write ("Exiting from the loop!");

//-->
</script>

</body>
</html>
```

The result of this result is as:

```
Navigator Object Properties
serviceWorker
webkitPersistentStorage
webkitTemporaryStorage
geolocation
doNotTrack
onLine
languages
language
```

```
userAgent
product
platform
appVersion
appName
appCodeName
hardwareConcurrency
maxTouchPoints
vendorSub
vendor
productSub
cookieEnabled
mimeTypes
plugins
javaEnabled
getStorageUpdates
getGamepads
webkitGetUserMedia
vibrate
getBattery
sendBeacon
registerProtocolHandler
unregisterProtocolHandler
Exiting from the loop
```

In all of these control statements used, the use of the break statement is very important to all of them. It is where it comes out of the loop by freeing itself from the enclosure. This technique is used ideally in situations where the user wants to leave the loop without reaching the end.

The interpreter is instructed by the continue statement to commence the following action while jumping over the code available at that moment.

This means that when faced with a continue statement, the movement of the program directs to the loop expression check at once.

When the output is still true, it proceeds to the next action. If the output is false, it simply dislodges from the loop.

An example of this is as follows:

```
<html>
<body>
<script type="text/javascript">
<!—
var x = 1;
document.write("Entering the loop<br /> ");
while (x < 10)
{
x = x + 1;
if (x == 5){
continue; // skill rest of the loop body
}
document.write( x + "<br />");

}
document.write("Exiting the loop!<br /> ");
//-->
</script>
<p>Set the variable to different value and then try...</p>
</body>
</html>
```

The resulting output of this is as follows:

feeding the loop

2

3

4

6

7

8

9

10

Exiting the loop!

For the break statement example is as follows:

```html
<html>

<body>

<script type="text/javascript">

<!--
var x = 1;

document.write("Entering the loop<br /> ");

while (x < 20)
{

if (x == 5){

break; // breaks out of loop completely
}

x = x + 1;

document.write( x + "<br />");
}

document.write("Exiting the loop!<br /> ");
//-->
</script>

</body>
</html>
```

The resulting output from this is as follows:

Entering the loop
2
3
4
5
Exiting the loop!

Chapter 4: JavaScript functions

JavaScript functions are known as the core of JavaScript and are very significant. Tying a program with value is put into very many uses. One significant way is enabling its users to be able to arrange bugger programs, lessen repetitiveness, to align given names with their partners and to separate said partners as well. Another use of functions is giving meaning to fresh concepts. In language, coming up with new words is cumbersome, this however is not the case in JavaScript which thrives in this.

Anyone who can speak English fluently has a lot of vocabulary under their belt at any one time. The same is not true for programs with very few ones having the same numbers in them. The words and phrases used by programming languages are also very rigid and do not leave room for manipulation like say the English language does.

This is why programming languages allow creation of fresh vocabulary to reduce chances of it getting too repetitive.

Therefore a function is a group statement that can be executed to perform a particular task in a program. A function allows the user to eliminate the possibility of repetitiveness which is very annoying and tedious. A function is also equipped with the ability to split up a larger program into smaller pieces that are easier to handle and utilize.

JavaScript is enabled with characters that allow it to compose code from functions. An example is document.write( ) , write( ) is a function which is been used again and again since it has been written in core JavaScript only once.

4.1 Function Definition

In other words, a function can well be described as binding in which its value is what is called a function. The code below is a good example as it illustrates a function that outputs the square of a certain number.

```
const square = function(x) {
return x * x;
};
console.log(square(8));
// → 64
```

A user must always describe a function right before putting it into use. One design to understand a function is utilizing the important words of the function which is pursued by then the name of the function, parameters which can either be full or empty, ending with a block statement with curly braces.

It is worth noting that it is common for a function to contain a number of parameters of having no parameters whatsoever. A sample of this is 'chewgum' is a function that doesn't display any parameter while on the other hand 'happy' has a number of them.

```
const makeNoise = function() {
console.log("Pling!");
};
makeNoise();
// → Pling!
const power = function(base, exponent) {
let result = 1;
for (let count = 0; count < exponent; count++) {
result *= base;
}
return result;
};
console.log(power(2, 10));
// → 1024
```

There are functions that are able to output values which include square and happy whereas others are not able to. A point to note is the amount of function that comes back is determined by that of the return statement. At the point where such a function and control happen on each other, it escapes the given functions with the return amount to the specific code that summoned the function. An undefined function will be as a result of a keyword that came back lacking an expression. An example of a return statement of functions that come back lacking is described an undefined.

The code in the function does not give the first values. These are given by the function that called parameters to it behaving more like regular bindings.

4.2 Binding and scopes

Every binging contains a scope that is a portion of the program of which its transparency is complete. The scope can be said to be the total program when bindings are described on the outside of a function and a user can access them at any time they need them. These are global functions as we learnt earlier. Local functions are the ones designed to be stated on the inner of a function that cannot be useful outside of it in any way, shape or form.

Always when a function is summoned, moments of fresh bindings are realized which in a way avails a way for functions to do isolated leading to functions exist individually in their smaller areas (local) without much awareness or effect from the outside area (global).

To avail bindings with const and let means they will be local to the group that they are availed in and each created within any loop will have the code coming at the start and end of it not be able to view it. In older versions of JavaScript, functions were the only ones charged with the mandate to come up with fresh scopes meaning aged bindings which were formed with the keyword var can be seen in all the functions they are in.

They can also be seen worldwide when not within the function at all as well.

```
let a = 5;
if (true) {
let b = 10;
var c= 20;
console.log (a + b + c);
// → 35
}
// y is not visible here
console.log (a + c);
// → 25
```

Each scope could have other scopes view near it resulting in a viewable in the group in the example given. This is untrue in the event that a collection of bindings share names that mean the code views those within. Take a sample where the available code attests to p within a function this means it will not be possibly for it to view its p because it will only be enabled to view its P and not the global p.

It is possible for each scope to look within the scope meaning x will only be seen within the block in accordance with the sample provided. Differences occur only when bindings a number of them are given a similar name meaning the code is only able to view the one at the most inside point.

A sample can be explained when the situated code within the function half calls n because this means it is only viewing its very own n and not the universal n.

```
const halve = function(p) {
return p / 2;
};
let p = 5;
console.log(halve(25));
// → 12.5
console.log(p);
// → 5
```

4.3 Calling a Function

For you to be in apposition to call a function, you have to type its name then call it.

```
<html>
<head>
<script type="text/javascript">
function sayHello()
{
document.write ("Hello there!");
}
</script>
</head>
<body>
<p>Click the following button to call the function</p>
<form>
<input type="button" onclick="sayHello()" value="Say Hello">
</form>
<p>Use different text in write method and then try...</p>
</body>
</html>
```

In the provided example above, there is a function named 'sayHello' . There's a button indented to Say Hello as you can see and an on click attribute which calls the function. By pressing a button, you summon a function followed by processing what it contains in it.

Now we keenly observe the provided example as well which is said to be a program charged with the mandate of making calls of a few functions:

```
function greet(who) {
console.log("Hello " + who);
}
greet("Harry");
console.log("Bye");
```

Going through the program simply would be similar to the 'greet' call which will result in the skip to control in line two to the beginning of the function The function have to call console.log, which will control and do its required task, before reversing control to the second line. Once accomplished it will move to the end of the greet function and therefore returns to the previous place that first named it (line 4). After naming, the line will console.log once more. After returning, the program will end.

Of importance is for the PC to be able to remember the point at which the call came through because it is important to note that a function must jump to its initial position which is the one that placed the call in the first place.

Therefore the console.log has to return to say hallo to the function after it is done. In a similar manner it will go back to the program's point of ending as well. The point of the call stack is the storage area in the computer where all this info is saved. The info still in use will be stored above the context whenever there is naming of a function.

Whenever any function comes back to the point where it started, it has to rid itself of the details at the top of the stack and also make use of it while continuing its execution as well.

In order to save this context, you must have enough memory in your computer therefore check on it before you start to avoid inconveniences. When the context stored is large in quantitiy, your computer will inform you by displaying messages indication stack memory is full therefore you have to free up more space in order to keep working smoothly.

The code provided for you below is a clear indication of this because it asks a question which is very hard to your computer and as a result there is a chain between the two functions that go back and forth.

In case computers had limitless stack memory, then this would go on and on with no end in sight. This is why it is important for stack memory to be limited:

```
function chicken() {
return egg();
}
function egg() {
return chicken();
}
console.log(chicken() + " came first.");
// → ??
```

4.4 Declaration of function

This is known as a simpler and easier way to create a binding of a function as needed even though it functions in a different way when the keyword of the function is utilized at the statement starting point.

```
function square(x) {
return x * x;
}
```

The above is a sample of a declaration of a function. It is characterized by the definition of the square connection point at every function that is given. It is simpler to code due to the fact that it does not make use of the semicolon which is to come after the function. Still it is important to note one exception of this format of definition of the function that is important to note.

```
console.log("The future says:", future());
function future() {
return "You'll never have flying cars";
}
```

Still the resulting function that comes below the code preceding the code must also work. It is important to note that declarations of functions are not normally characterized by an ability to participate in the top to bottom regular control of movement. They are in concept transferred to the top and are utilized in code within the scope. This is of importance because it gives you the freedom to ask for code in a way that is oriented in results not minding the definition of all functions at the start before their utilization.

4.5 Function Parameters

This code displayed below is known to be executed without any hitches whatsoever:

```
function square(x) { return x * x; }
console.log(square(4, true, "hedgehog"));
// → 16
```

It is called with three despite it being defined square only with one parameter and the language used in no way complains. This is because of its ability to assume arguments in their numbers and be able to use the square at the beginning.

There is liberty in JavaScript when it comes to a few cases which you will come by while using a function at certain times. An example of this is when you put a large number of arguments, the excess ones will be assumed. When a few arguments are used the parameters that are missing will get attached to the value which is undefined at the moment. The only problem here is that a moment will come when numbers that are wrong will be able to pass through the function as well. This is not under discussion.

The plus side to this is the behavior utilized which allows functions naming by arguments that are different in numbers. An example of this is the function minus which will not be able to copy the operator through acting on arguments that are one or another.

```
function minus(a, b) {
if (b === undefined) return -a;
else return a - b;console.log(minus(10));
// → -10
console.log(minus(10, 5));
// → 5
46
```

In the case where an = is placed as an operator of a parameter and will later have an expression follow it, the unknown argument will be replaced by the value expression.

A sample of such a power version will therefore be indicative of making the argument that comes second of no use.

When there is no provision or pass of the undefined value, break down will result in two resulting in what will; be a square.

```
function power(base, exponent = 2) {
let result = 1;
for (let count = 0; count < exponent; count++) {
result *= base;
}
return result;
}
console.log(power(4));
// → 16
console.log(power(2, 6));
// → 64
```

As we proceed ahead, we will witness a path through which the body of a function will be able to get to the list which is whole of the arguments in the very case it might have been passed. This is of importance due to the fact that it enables a function to allow a number of arguments at any moment which are required.

The example of this is as below:

```
console.log does this—it outputs all of the values it is given.
console.log("C", "O", 2);
// → C O 2
```

The ones that have seen functions lacking parameters in them are the ones known as now. Still it is worth noting that there is the presence of the option to leave behind a number of parameters in the creation of a function.

The parameters left behind have the option of being captured within manipulations where a function can be completed above them also. Capacities have the ability to take up a variety of parameters in the off chance they find themselves in isolation due to the use of the comma. Below is a case that is indicative of this:

```html
<html>
<head>
<script type="text/javascript">
function sayHello(name, age)
{
document.write (name + " is " + age + " years old.");
}
</script>
</head>
<body>
<p>Click the following button to call the function</p>
<form>
<input type="button" onclick="sayHello('Zara', 7)" value="Say Hello">
</form>

</body>
</html>
```

4.6 Bindings and scope

There is what is called a degree in every single coupling which is known as the portion of the program where the coupling is in full view and seen completely. The ties which are symbolized in the outer part of capacity or square are the program in its totality at the degree point and you can be able to make use of such ties in any point at which you are provided for. They are ones that are referred to as worldwide.

The same cannot be said for parameter functions made in the inner parts of a function because they are ones that are known as bindings that are local. They are only referenced within the function as a rule.

Whenever the capacity is summoned, there is a creation of new samples of all these. This will result in some lack of connection between capacities because every capacity will be summoned to function in its own limited environment (which is similar to saying its own home neighborhood) and will be able to understand on a regular basis even with little knowledge of all that is going on in the world outside of it at all times.

Const and let is made use of to proclaim ties which are in near locations to the square in which their announcement, the code below and after the circle will not be able to view it even with stretching of the imaginative.

Before the year 2015, adaptations of JavaScript new extensions were made meaning the ties in the olden days which were created with the catch phrase var were easy to notice in the entire capacity which came up in the degree which is global in the off chance that they were not at capacity as well.

The above is well displayed below:

```
let x = 10;
if (true) {
let y = 20;
var z = 30;
console.log(x + y + z);
// → 60
}
// y is not visible here
console.log(x + z);
// → 40
```

There is the ability for all extensions to "watch out" following their being surrounded by the degree as long as they along the line x which can be viewed in the inside of the square in the model that is given. The only case that can be said to be special is only when ties that are variety have similarities in terms of their names. Here within such lines the code is allowed to make use of only the one that is deepest. An example is a code within the capacity that is divided escapes to n and this will result in it viewing only its own n and will not be able to see the n which is global.

Below is a model indicative of this:

```
const halve = function(n) {
return n / 2;
};
let n = 10;

console.log(halve(100));
// → 50
console.log(n);
// → 10
```

4.7 Nested Functions

In the days leading up to the creation of 1.2 JavaScript, the definition of work was only allowed at the highest level across the world. But when 1.2 JavaScript became a reality, there was room for the definitions to now be handled within a variety of more local settings as well. Still this is marred by limitations in some ways with definitions of capacity because there is an indication they may be a no show within of circles or even in conditionals at all.

The hindrances experienced on definitions of capacities still should be known that they are limited to announcements of work with the explanation of capacity.

Together with the fact that JavaScript is created with the capability to be distinguishable on a global scale plus to squares and capacities that are tied closer as well have the capabilities to be created within capacities and squares which will result in the production of a large number of degrees inside of them in a given area.

As a sample, here is a capacity that has the ability to produce the expected fixings in order to create a hummus clamp and is able to have another capacity included within it as well:

```
const hummus = function(factor) {
const ingredient = function(amount, unit, name) {
let ingredientAmount = amount * factor;
if (ingredientAmount > 1) {
unit += "s";
}
console.log(`${ingredientAmount} ${unit} ${name}`);
};
ingredient(1, "can", "chickpeas");
ingredient(0.25, "cup", "tahini");
ingredient(0.25, "cup", "lemon juice");
ingredient(1, "clove", "garlic");
ingredient(2, "tablespoon", "olive oil");
ingredient(0.5, "teaspoon", "cumin");
};
```

The main factor that comes from the capacity that is external is able to be viewed by the code within the capacity which is fixing it even with the possibility that the ties which are nearest to it as a sample sum fixing or unit cannot be mistaken in the capacity which is external even with the imagination stretched. The way in which the ties have been arranged that cannot be mistaken within the square is in the control of the spot that is accurate within the said square within the message program as was. It is also possible for extensions that are near as well to view the scopes of the whole neighborhood containing it including the degrees as well which are able to view the extension that is worldwide. Perusing that is lexical is the way to handle percievability that is viewed as restrictive. Later on in the parts that accompany this, more will be discussed inj terms of literals that are of work which are part of 1.2 JavaScript as well and have the capability to present themselves in any articulation of JavaScript which means they are able to present themselves within if and in proclamations that are different as well. The model that accompanies this is made use of by capacities that have settled in actualization as priority:

```
<html>
<head>
<script type="text/javascript">
<!--
function hypotenuse(a, b) {
function square(x) { return x*x; }
return Math.sqrt(square(a) + square(b));
}
function secondFunction(){
var result;
result = hypotenuse(1,2);
document.write ( result );
}
//-->
</script>
</head>
<body>
<p>Click the following button to call the function</p>
<form>
<input type="button" onclick="secondFunction()" value="Call Function">
</form>
</body>
</html>
```

4.8 Constructor of functions

A capacity can be characterized by anyone for its ability to utilize a function progressively () by making use of a constructor of function hand in hand with the administrator who is new.

Below we view the structure of linguistics made use of by a constructor function that utilizes capacity hand in hand with the administrator who is new as well.

```
<script type="text/javascript">
<!--
var variablename = new Function(Arg1, Arg2..., "Function Body");
//-->
</script>
```

It is the work of the constructor to manage the number of contentions of string at all times. The capacity's body is the very end of contention and is able to have articulations of JavaScript that are said to be discretionary and can therefore be kept from each other by making use of semicolons.

Please note that the constructor function does not in any way pass any arguments which have been given a specific name for the created function.

It is the function lacking a name that has been created with the constructor of function that is called the functions that are anonymous.

```html
<html>
<head>
<script type="text/javascript">
<!--
var func = new Function("x", "y", "return x*y;");
function secondFunction(){
var result;
result = func(10,20);
document.write ( result );
}
//-->
</script>
</head>
<body>
<p>Click the following button to call the function</p>
<form>
<input type="button" onclick="secondFunction()" value="Call Function">
</form>
<p>Use different parameters inside the function and then try...</p>
</body>
</html>
```

4.9Literals of functions

A literal of functions is so called because it is an expression charged with the mandate to define a function lacking in a name.

There is a similarity of the syntax used by the literal functions and that used by the statement of functions. Still it is worth noting that it is made use of as an articulation and not as an announcement and still there is a lack of name of capacity even with the imagination being stretched.

```
<script type="text/javascript">
<!--

var variablename = function(Argument List){
Function Body
};
//-->
</script>
```

Still it is worth noting that you are in a position to pin point a name of a function even when making a function that is literal.

This can be best viewed as below even though there is no significance in the name and it has no value:

```
<script type="text/javascript">
<!--
var variablename = function FunctionName(Argument List){
Function Body
};
//-->
</script>
```

Still it is worth noting that a restricted capacity has the ability to still obtain a name for a portion of the program being run. In such an occurrence which inly happens at one time and it is never allowed to indicate that it wants it to occur again. This is exactly why it is so simple to mess with the capacity together with the name it is given even though both of them have been described to have their differences. Still a worthy capacity is able to perform all the things that the qualities that are different can do as well. This is indicative of your ability to make use of it in a manner that asserts to the self in terms of articulations therefore there is simply not just a call. Therefore it is possible for esteem of a capacity to be stored within another authoritative and still be able to display it as a capacity to a contention etc.

In the same manner, a capacity held by a coupling should be noted as only an official that is customary and is possible to have it doled by another when it is not steady enough. This is indicated here:

```
let launchMissiles = function() {
missileSystem.launch("now");
};
if (safeMode) {

launchMissiles = function() {/* do nothing */};
}
```

The utilization of the literals of function is displayed in the example given below:

```
<html>
<head>
<script type="text/javascript">
<!--
var func = function(x,y){ return x*y };
function secondFunction(){
var result;
result = func(10,20);
document.write ( result );
}
//-->
</script>
</head>
<body>

<p>Click the following button to call the function</p>
<form>
<input type="button" onclick="secondFunction()" value="Call Function">
</form>
<p>Use different parameters inside the function and then try...</p>
</body>
</html>
```

4.10 Functions of arrow

A unique capacity of documentation which differs from the others described a while back is the third one. Different from the watchword capacity, the documentation makes ues of a bolt (=>) which is created by a sign that equals and an administrator that equals as well and is created by >=).

```
const power = (base, exponent) => {
let result = 1;
for (let count = 0; count < exponent; count++) {
result *= base;
}
return result;
};
```

The ones pursuant to the parameters that are run down are the bolts followed closely by the body of the capacity. The communication transmitted is like "this info (the parameters) creates this outcome (the body)". In the case where the named parameter is only one you are allowed to not include the enclosures that surround the list of parameter as well. When the body is an articulation that is said to be solitary and not in a square in props, it is possible for the articulation to resume from the capacity as well. Therefore the two definitions of square have similar functions and a model if this is well displayed below:

```
const square1 = (x) => { return x * x; };
const square2 = x => x * x;
When an arrow function has no parameters at all, its parameter list is just
an empty set of parentheses.
const horn = () => {
console.log("Toot");
};
```

In all honesty there is no one great need of having the two (capacities that are bolt and capacities that are articulations) within the language at the very same moment. In 2015, bolt capacities were inclusive in order to be able to work and have the capacity to create small capacities of articulations in a manner which can be said to be as little verbose as possible.

4.11 The return statement

JavaScript is said to have capacities within it that are said to have a return that is discretionary. This is important because you may at one time need to restore from a capacity a certain incentive. Still it is important to note that this is the announcement that is final in articulation in a capacity.

An example is you can be able to put through two numbers in capacity and afterwards know in anticipation that the capacity can be able to restore in your program calling their augmentation as well.

The model that accompanies this here below, a capacity is characterized in a way that gets two parameters and in turn connects them before restoration of the resultant in the program calling.

This is indicated as follows:

```
<html>
<head>
<script type="text/javascript">
function concatenate(first, last)
{
var full;
full = first + last;
return full;
}
function secondFunction()
{
var result;
result = concatenate('Zara', 'Ali');
document.write (result );
}
</script>
</head>

<body>
<p>Click the following button to call the function</p>
<form>
<input type="button" onclick="secondFunction()" value="Call Function">
</form>
<p>Use different parameters inside the function and then try...</p>
</body>
</html>
```

4.12 Summary

For capacities to be brought to programs of PCs there are two ways that are said to be regular. The initial one is where you wind up creating code that can be compared in a number of instances again and again and therefore you should take care not to lean this way at all. The more code used means the more the chance for mistakes to be stored within a probability and material that is increasingly perusable for people trying to understand the program.

Therefore, obtaining the usefulness that is rehashed, getting a name that is descent for it and it is placed to capacity is the main thing.

The only other way is by you discovering that you recquire usefulness some of it that had not been composed by you at this point and therefore is merited by its own capacity as well. Start then by giving the capacity a name and follow this up with the defining of its body as well. You can even start composition of code that utilizes the capacity even ahead of characterizing the actual capacity.

The problem will be in finding a name that is descent for a capacity which is an indication of the exact concept you are trying to wrap. Below is a case indicative of all of these.

Here the concept is to create a program with the capability to produce two numbers at the very same time. This will be the number of goats and chicken within a farm followed by the words goats and chicken with cushioning of zeros before the two numbers making them three digits every time.

- 007 Goats

- 011 Chickens

This requires two contentious components which are the number of goats in totality and the number of chickens in totality as well. Let us start composing the code: This requests a component of two contentions—the number of goats and the number of chickens.

```
function printFarmInventory(cows, chickens) {
let cowString = String(cows);
while (cowString.length < 3) {
cowString = "0" + cowString;
}
console.log(`${cowString} Cows`);
let chickenString = String(chickens);
while (chickenString.length < 3) {
chickenString = "0" + chickenString;
}
console.log(`${chickenString} Chickens`);
}
printFarmInventory(7, 11);
```

The length of a string as required after that same string has been articulated is obtained from the process of composition. On the other hand, it is the duty of the circles of while to keep emitting numerical of string to the point they find themselves in the event of three characters in length. This can be seen as a great strategy. Still it is worth noting since we are to send the code to the rancher together with their bill, she may along the way call to inform us that she has added more pigs to her numbers and can we be able to stretch the product out to include her added numbers as well. This too is possible for us to do for the rancher.

We first need to stop and reevaluate our progress before we set forth to reorder the four lines and still we need to find a much better and to the point way of achieving all of these.

It will look something like this:

```
function printZeroPaddedWithLabel(number, label) {
let numberString = String(number);
while (numberString.length < 3) {
numberString = "0" + numberString;
}
console.log(`${numberString} ${label}`);
}
function printFarmInventory(cows, chickens, pigs) {
printZeroPaddedWithLabel(cows, "Cows");
printZeroPaddedWithLabel(chickens, "Chickens");
printZeroPaddedWithLabel(pigs, "Pigs");
}
printFarmInventory(7, 11, 3);
It works! But that name, printZeroPaddedWithLabel, is a little awkward.
It conflates three things—printing, zero-padding, and adding a label—into a
single function.
Instead of lifting out the repeated part of our program wholesale, let's try
to pick out a single concept.
function zeroPad(number, width) {
let string = String(number);
while (string.length < width) {
string = "0" + string;
}
return string;
}
function printFarmInventory(cows, chickens, pigs) {
console.log(`${zeroPad(cows, 3)} Cows`);
console.log(`${zeroPad(chickens, 3)} Chickens`);
console.log(`${zeroPad(pigs, 3)} Pigs`);
}
printFarmInventory(7, 16, 3);
```

Naming the capacity with a name that is more appealing as well as pleasing like zeroPad enables a user who is going through it at any time to be able to understand it completely with little effort. The capacity then becomes of so much value in the end even more than the expressed program. An example can be you using it to enable you to print number tables that can be said to be very easy to make adjustments to.

It is important to consider how much flexibility and keenness should be in possession of the capacities we are using. It is possible to choose to just make any composition using a capacity that is very basic (enabled to only cushion any numeral to be 3 characters) to just any number summation in its convulsion in a framework design which is the one to handles numbers that are said to be fragmented, numbers that are said to be negative, decimal spots arrangements as well as various characters that need cushioning as well.

The only time to include any form of cunningness in a guideline that is very significant is when you are very sure that you absolutely need it. It can be alluring to you to keep composing systems that are basic and general for usefulness run over by you. Still do not fall prey to such temptations because it will not lead you to be able to complete work in any form that is genuine.

This means all the code you will be composing will ultimately be of no use at all/

Functions that are high ordered

A program that is said to be expansive is a very big program and can take a very long time to compose to the end. The size which is right has to include a nature that is multifaceted and this can confound engineers of software because it is very confounding. Engineers of software who find themselves confused have a way of producing bugs that are mixed up inside of the projects they present. This is why a program that is very big offers a wide amount of spacing for the inclusion of bugs making it very difficult to trace them and get rid of them.

As fast as possible let us resume cases that were two in the past presentation the first being independent and with a length of six.

It was presented as:

```
let total = 0, count = 1;
while (count <= 10) {
total += count;
count += 1;
}
console.log(total);
```

The 2nd one is dependent on capacities which are two in number on the outside and can be a long line only.

console.log(sum(range(1, 10)));

It is worth noting that there is a possibility for this to contain a bug in it.

The resulting program can be said to be very bug by simply checking the size of the range and total meaning . It can be said to be even greater than the very first one. Still you can accept this as a fact at face value. This can be done on the base that the arrangement communicated has to be in jargon relevant to the problem that is the one being explained at hand. The summarization of number scopes is not only about counters and circles but also about aggregates and reaches being used up as well.

The ultimate jargon meanings which are the range and the aggregate capacities, have to at all-time be inclusive of counters, circles and other subtleties that can be said to be coincidental within as well. They are said to be very simple to get them right since their communication is of ideas that are less difficult. Capacities that are said to work on different capacities are the ones that are referred to higher request and this can be by either accepting them as being contentious or by simply taking them back.

There is no exceptional point as to how such capacities exist since we have already described capacities as being normal. This is obtained from science where the capacities differentiation and their quality differences as well is paid more attention to on an increased basis.

Capacities that are of a higher request nature permit over activities to be digested and this does not apply to only those of qualities. Still the structures they come in are few. A sample of this is when we have capacities charged with the mandate of creating new capacities as outlined below:

```
function greaterThan(n) {
return m => m > n;
}
let greaterThan10 = greaterThan(10);
console.log(greaterThan10(11));
// → true
```
And we can have functions that change other functions.
```
function noisy(f) {
return (...args) => {
console.log("calling with", args);
let result = f(...args);
console.log("called with", args, ", returned", result);
return result;
};
}
noisy(Math.min)(3, 2, 1);
// → calling with [3, 2, 1]
// → called with [3, 2, 1] , returned 1
```
We can even write functions that provide new types of control flow.
```
function unless(test, then) {
if (!test) then();
}
```

```
repeat(3, n => {
unless(n % 2 == 1, () => {
console.log(n, "is even");
});
});
// → 0 is even
// → 2 is even
```
There is a built-in array method, forEach, that provides something like a for/of loop as a higher-order function.
```
["A", "B"].forEach(l => console.log(l));
// → A
// → B
```

Chapter 5: JavaScript Objects

In Programming, there is something many refer to as an article arranged to programme. This is a lot of systems that utilization questions as the focal guideline of program association. Article situated programming has molded the plan of many programming dialects. This incorporates the language of JavaScript. This section will endeavor to depict the manner in which similar ideas can find their application within JavaScript.

5.1 Encapsulating

The thought that can be said to be the real one in item arranged is to partition programs into smaller pieces making each piece in charge of dealing with its very own state at some random time.

Various bits of such a program communicate with one another through a procedure known interfaces which are constrained arrangements of capacities or ties that give helpful usefulness at an increasingly conceptual level, concealing their accurate usage.

Such program pieces are displayed utilizing objects as they were. Their interface comprises of explicit arrangements of techniques and properties that they use. Components said to be portions of the interface are the ones referred to as open. Still the other ones are referred to as code that is outside and is not to be contacted and is therefore named private.

Languages in their numbers give an opportunity for the recognition of private from open and therefore stop any code from the outside from being able to access the ones that are private by any means necessary.

By and by, JavaScript is adopting the moderate strategy, doesn't do this—not yet at any rate.

There is as of now work in progress to add this to the language yet it is yet to be finished. Regardless of the way in which the language is in a deficit of such a qualification that is to be worked on, engineers of JavaScript are using such thoughts very effectively in the present times. the interface that is accessible on a regular basis is said to be displayed either in the remarks or in the documents. Also it is worth noting the importance of on a regular basis placing the underscore at the names of property start point in order to clearly show that such properties are the ones that are private. Furthermore, isolating interfaces from usage is an extremely good thought. It is normally called exemplification.

Here is a summary of an object oriented programming language capabilities. It includes the following:

- **Encapsulation:** in other words this can clearly be described as the ability to store information said to be related in data form or method form within an object.
- **Aggregating:** This can be said in simpler terms to be the ability for the storage of an object on the inside of yet another object.
- **Inheritance:** This can be described as the ability of a class to get reliant on yet another class or in other cases a number of classes for the case of some of its methods and properties as well.
- **Polymorphism:** This can be described as the ability to write a method or a function that is able to work in ways that are numerous and not only in just one way.

5.2 Inheritance

A few frameworks are known to be symmetric grids.

This can be irregardless of even if you place a framework that is symmetric to reflect in the area surrounding its top left to base askew, it no doubt will be constant in equivalence. On the other hand, the worth put away at x,y is consistently equivalent to that at y,x. Envision you need an information structure like Matrix however one that authorizes the network is and stays even consistently.

You could compose it without any preparation despite the fact that that would include rehashing some code fundamentally the same as what we previously composed previously. In this way it is excessively redundant.

JavaScript's model framework makes it conceivable to make another class, much like the old class. We will examine classes in the following sub-section however definitions being fairly new in terms of portions of the utilized properties.

The new class model is gotten from the model that is old yet includes another definition, state, the set technique.

The terms of programming within the arranged items are what is fondly referred to as a legacy with the newest class acquiring properties as well as conducts from the class in the past.

```
class SymmetricMatrix extends Matrix {
constructor(size, element = (x, y) => undefined) {
super(size, size, (x, y) => {
if (x < y) return element(y, x);
else return element(x, y);
});
}
set(x, y, value) {
super.set(x, y, value);
if (x != y) {
super.set(y, x, value);
}
}
}

let matrix = new SymmetricMatrix(5, (x, y) => `${x},${y}`);
console.log(matrix.get(2, 3));
// → 3,2
```

The utilization of the word expands implies that the particular class is not allowed to be founded in a straight forward manner on the model which is object default on a class that is said to be different. Such kind of class is what is known as the superclass. The inferred class is what is known as the subclass.

In Order to instate a Symmetric Matrix occasion, the constructor just calls its superclass' constructor through the super watchword. This is fundamentally provided that this new item is to carry on (generally) like a Matrix, it will require the occurrence properties that lattices contain in them. To guarantee the network is balanced, the constructor needs to wrap the component work so as to swap the directions for qualities underneath the inclining.

Once more, the set technique utilizes super but at the present moment it is not to place a call to the one constructing but to call a strategy that is very particular from the strategies arrangements that are known to be of a superclass.

Presently there is thought on redoing set but still there is a need for the utilization of the conduct that was the initial one first.

It is worth noting that such a set can allude to the strategy that is the newest one meaning no calling can work at all. There is an approach to techniques of calling of super which was their characterization within the superclass inside class strategies.

Legacy enables us to manufacture somewhat various information types from existing information types without breaking a sweat. It is an essential piece of the article arranged a custom, nearby exemplification and polymorphism and keeping in mind that the last two are presently commonly viewed as great thoughts, legacy is a progressively dubious thought.

Still when the polymorphism and being embodied can be made use of in the separation of code bits from each other, which will in turn reduce them being so tangled together within the program in general will enable legacy to in general sense tie together classes which will only result in more tangles as well. When you get from any class you must on a regular basis discover the way in which it functions which is different from the way in which you are making use of it.

A legacy can be a proficient instrument, and you should utilize it occasionally in your own projects in spite of the fact that it shouldn't be the principal device you connect for, and you most likely shouldn't effectively go searching for chances to build class orders (family trees of classes) too.

5.3 Polymorphism

When calling upon the String capacity (this is one that changes over an incentive of any string) for any item, the strategy called upon is the toString one which will in turn make trials to create a string that is significant from it. It is important still to note that the standards models potion will enable the characterization of their own version of toString in a manner through which they can create a string containing data that can be said to be of more value than that of "[object Object]".

All of these can be done on a sole basis.

```
Rabbit.prototype.toString = function() {
return `a ${this.type} rabbit`;
};
console.log(String(blackRabbit));
// → a black rabbit
```

This is a straightforward occasion of an influential thought springing up. In the chance where some code is written to function with things that are specified in terms of their interface which by the way here are the toString technique meaning article in any format that is helpful to the interface has the ability to be connected with the code being used and can also function as well.

Such a method is the one that alludes to polymorphism. Code that is polymorphic is able to function with estimations in a variety of shapes the only need being they are able to back up the interface to be helped. You can likewise add this interface to your very own items too! However, before we can do that, we have to recognize what images are (characterize images).

Regularly articles are made out of characteristics. In the event that a trait contains a capacity, it is viewed as a strategy for the article; generally the characteristic is viewed as property.

5.4 Object Method

These can be described in simple terms as properties charged with the mandate to collect values of functions and as an example, the one below clearly displays this:

```
let rabbit = {};
rabbit.speak = function(line) {
console.log(`The rabbit says '${line}'`);
};
rabbit.speak("I'm alive.");
// → The rabbit says 'I'm alive.'
```

To include more subtleties, strategies are the capacities that given the item a chance to accomplish something or let something done to it. The distinction between a capacity and a technique is that capacity is an independent unit of proclamations while a strategy is joined to an item and can be referenced by this catchphrase.

Generally a strategy needs to accomplish something with the item it was approached in any case. At this point capacity is summoned as a strategy and can look up just like property and come quickly in a manner similar to object.method ().

```
function speak(line) {

console.log(`The ${this.type} rabbit says '${line}'`);
}

let whiteRabbit = {type: "white", speak};

let hungryRabbit = {type: "hungry", speak};

whiteRabbit.speak("Oh my ears and whiskers, " +
"how late it's getting!");

// → The white rabbit says 'Oh my ears and whiskers, how

// late it's getting!'

hungryRabbit.speak("I could use a carrot right now.");
// → The hungry rabbit says 'I could use a carrot right now.'
```

Take this into consideration as an added parameter to be passed in a way that is different also. Therefore, when there is a need for you to pass it in a manner that is explicit, you can make use of a method for calling functions that obtains the values as the argument that is first and the arguments to follow are treated as parameters that are normal.

speak.call(hungryRabbit, "Burp!");

Given that each capacity has its own this official, whose worth relies upon the manner in which it is called, you can't allude to the this of the enveloping degree by an ordinary capacity characterized with the capacity catchphrase.

Bolt capacities are diverse on the grounds that they don't tie their own this yet can see this official of the degree around them.

5.5 Properties of Objects

These properties of items can be of the types of information said to be crude and three in number. Generally they are factors that are utilized inside in the items techniques, however can likewise be comprehensively unmistakable factors that are utilized all through the page.

Structure of linguistic for property addition to any article can be described as follows:

```
objectName.objectProperty =propertyValue;
```

A good example is:

var book= document. author;

To change the estimation of an article's number, consistently utilize a straightforward task proclamation, the Same way you'd appoint an incentive to a plain factor.

deal3.cost = 79.95;

Whatever the estimation of deal3.cost was, presently is 79.95, obviously, you could dole out a string rather than a number.

```
deal3.name = "Super-saver;
```

Whatever the estimation of deal3.name was, presently it's "Super-saver". You could likewise allocate a cluster rundown to a property.

```
deal3.features = ["Guarantee", "Free Ship"];
```

Whatever the estimation of deal3.features were, presently it's an exhibit with the components

"Assurance" and "Free Ship." You can likewise relegate a Boolean worth.

```
deal3.membersOnly = false;
```

Whatever the estimation of deal3.membersOnly was, presently it's false, you can likewise utilize a task articulation to characterize another property for an item. Assume the article deal3 had a few properties, yet none of them were deal3.market. Presently you need to include it, while doling out it an incentive too.

```
deal3.market = "local";
```

A similar way you can make an indistinct variable by not relegating it worth, you can make an item with no properties. var deal4 = {};

On the off chance that you need to make a property now and appoint it a worth later, you can make it with an estimation of unclear.

```
deal3.market = vague;
```

Note that the catchphrase unclear isn't in quotes. Is anything but a string at all and you can erase a property of an item whenever.

```
erase deal3.market;
```

You can verify whether a property of an item exists in it. The gave proclamation tests whether there is such an unbelievable marvel as deal3.market and appoints the outcome (genuine or false) to the

variable propertyExists.

```
propertyExists = "showcase" in deal3;
```

There are sure things to note: One you could utilize any legitimate variable name rather than propertyExists.

The watchword in asks, "The property market is in the article deal3—genuine or false?"

The property market is in statements.

The article deal3 isn't in statements.

5.6 Derived Properties Overriding

In the case property is added to any item even if its availability is present within the model or it is not available, the said property has to be included in the article too. On the off chance that there was property as of now with a similar name in the model, this property will never again influence the item since it is currently taken cover behind the article's property that is their own.

```
Rabbit.prototype.teeth = "small";
console.log(killerRabbit.teeth);
// → small
killerRabbit.teeth = "long, sharp, and bloody";
console.log(killerRabbit.teeth);
// → long, sharp, and bloody
console.log(blackRabbit.teeth);
// → small


console.log(Rabbit.prototype.teeth);
// → small
```

The graph displays the outcome after running all the code. The models of objects and the rabbits lie at the back of the killer Rabbit in the form of background though which observation of the properties excluded in the item can be conducted as well.

Going beyond the properties in existence within a model can be a tedious task to say the least. As the model of the hare teeth clearly displays, abrogation can be made use of when intending to express properties in a manner that is remarkable still with a class that is conventionally occurring while the items that are uncommon are given a chance to take an incentive that is standard within the model as well.

Superseding is additionally utilized in giving the standard capacity and exhibit models an alternate toString strategy than the essential item model.

```
console.log(Array.prototype.toString ==
Object.prototype.toString);
// → false
console.log([1, 2].toString());
// → 1,2
```

Calling toString on a cluster gives an outcome like calling .join(",") on it—it places commas within the exhibited qualities. Objects to be called in a manner that is straight forward in a prototype.toString delivered to a string that is alternate in a cluster.

This sort of capacity will in no way be considerate of the exhibits because it will basically place the objects words and that of the sort name between the sections of squares.

```
console.log(Object.prototype.toString.call([1, 2]));
// → [object Array]
```

5.7 User –Defined Objects

Items that are characterized for clients are what are known as set components of articles that are super set or in other words are what is commonly referred to as objects which are descendants of an item.

The administrator who is new uses it to make occasions of an item. For an item to be made an occasion, the administrator who is new will be followed closely by the technique constructor. The model displayed below shows the strategies of the constructor which are Objects ( ), Array ( ) and Date( ).

```
var employee = new Object();
var books = new Array("C++", "Perl", "Java");
var day = new Date("August 15, 1947");
```

The constructor object ()

A capacity that is known to make and also instate an article is what is called a constructor. An uncommon capacity constructor is an item provided by JavaScript for the assembling of the article. The object estimation arrival is what is given to a variable.

The new item has a reference held by the variable. It is important to note that properties assigned to the article should not be mistaken for factors and are therefore not in use of the watchword var in any way.

The example that follows is a clear demonstration of how an object is created:

```
<html>
<head>
<title>User-defined objects</title>
<script type="text/javascript">
var book = new Object(); // Create the object
book.subject = "Javascript"; // Assign properties to the object

book.author = "Erick";
</script>
</head>
<body>
<script type="text/javascript">
document.write("Book name is : " + book.subject + "<br>");
document.write("Book author is : " + book.author + "<br>");
</script>
</body>
</html>
```

The output that is obtained from this is as below:

Book name is: JavaScript
Book author is : Erick.

Still the example that follows shows you clearly on how an object is created with a function that is described as user defined. The keyword here is utilized as a reference to the object that a function has been passed through also.

```
<html>
<head>
<title>User-defined objects</title>
<script type="text/javascript">
function book(title, author){
this.title = title;
this.author = author;
}
</script>
</head>
<body>
<script type="text/javascript">
var myBook = new book("Perl", "Mohtashim");
document.write("Book title is : " + myBook.title + "<br>");
document.write("Book author is : " + myBook.author + "<br>");
</script>
</body>
</html>
```

The resulting output is

Book name is: JavaScript
Book author is : Erick.

Chapter 6: Document Object Model

At the point when opening a site page in the program you want to utilize, the particular program recovers the page's HTML message and parses it on. At that point the program is said to develop a model of the structure's report and this model is utilized in drawing of the page on the interface for your viewing. One of the many toys of the program that is JavaScript is the portrayal of the archive and is stored in a sandbox.

A sandbox can be described as a structure of information that it is possible to make changes to as well as go through it too. It is a structure of information that is live since when an alteration to it is made, you can view the refreshing of the screen page in order to display the progress that has been attained. An object document talks with the archive of the HTML to be displayed in the specific window. The item of the document is known to have properties that are different which are to allow entry and adjustments to the content of reports as needed.

Therefore try and picture a document of HTML as a set of boxes nested together too.

<body> and </body> enclose other tags, which also have some other tags and below is an example of these:

```html
<!doctype html>
<html>
<head>
<title>My home page</title>
</head>
<body>
<h1>My home page</h1>
<p>Hello, I am Marijn and this is my home page.</p>
<p>I also wrote a book! Read it
<a href="http://eloquentjavascript.net">here</a>.</p>
</body>
</html>
```

This specific page is said to have the following structure:

- The structure of information is the one used by the program to communicate with the record in pursuit of this shape. In every crate an article is present which you can make connections with in order to make a discovery of things. A sample of this is the label given by HTML in which is communicates to or with content and boxes contained additionally.

The DOM (Document Object Model) is what is eluded in such a portrayal.

- The archive which is said to be restrictive on a global scale is the one that permits access to the articles. Its property of element reports for the speaking item of <html> tag. Every record of HTML has a body and a head as well together with properties of a body and head too which indicates these components.

6.1 Trees

Keep in mind the sentence structure trees as expressed before on in this book. Notice that their structures are like the structure of a program's report also. Every hub may allude to different hubs, youngsters, which thusly may have their very own kids subsequently. This sort Of shape is normal of settled structures where components can contain sub components that are like themselves.

We call an information structure a tree since it has a spreading structure in it, has no cycles (a hub may not contain itself, straightforwardly or in a roundabout way), and has a well-characterized single root also. On account of the DOM, document.documentElement it fills in as the root for it.

It is basic to take note of those trees to come up with a great deal in software engineering. Notwithstanding speaking to recursive structures, for example, HTML archives or projects, frequently they are utilized to keep up arranged arrangements of information since components can without much of a stretch be found and embedded more proficiently in a tree than in a level cluster.

A run of the mill tree has various types of hubs. The structure of a linguistic tree for the language of the egg has what is referred to as qualities, identifiers and hubs of application as well. Hubs of application may contain young ones even if the identifiers and qualities are known as leaves of in other words young fewer hubs.

The DOM is pursued by the one that equals it. Hubs for components, which speak to HTML labels, decide the structure of the record. They can have youngster hubs thus. An issue known for its genuineness depicting a similar hub is the document.body. A number of such children can be hubs of leaves as a sample which are content bits or hubs of remarks.

Each Document Object Model (DOM) article hub contains what is referred to as a property nodeType which has a number code that is used to recognize the hub of sort it is. Code 1 is what components contain which can also be characterized by the property that is consistent Node.ELEMENT_NODE. Hubs of content which talk to a portion of content that has been recorded obtain code 3 (Node.TEXT_NODE). Remarks have code 8 (Node.COMMENT_NODE).

It is worth noting that the DOM communicates with the report of the HTML displayed in the specified window. This object of the document has properties that are different and express to articles that are also different which grant permission to access as well as alter contents of reports.

The process used to obtain the report and how it is also altered is what is called the DOM.

Here is a short conclusion of the DOM:

- **Object window:** object window it the one located at the upper most part of the pyramid and is known to be the element that is outside of the object puramid as well.

- **Object document:** all documents of HTML that are to be loaded are what become an object document and it is the document that holds the items of a certain page as well.

- **Object form:** It is the place where all that is placed in between the <form>...</form> tags sets the object form.

- **Elements of form control:** It is the object of form that has the elements in totality which have been defined for this particular object inclusive of buttons, buttons of radio and fields of texts.

Diagrammatically the hierarchical structure can be designed and is illustrated below:

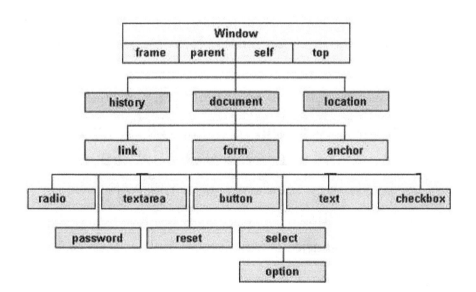

There a number of DOMs contained in JavaScript and they include:

- **The IE4 DOM**: This document object model was introduced in Version 4 of Microsoft's Internet Explorer browser. IE 5 and later versions include support for most basic W3C DOM features as well.

- **The Legacy DOM**: This is the model that was during the early versions of the JavaScript language. It is well supported by all browsers, but grants access only to certain key portions of documents, such as forms, form elements and images.

- **The W3C DOM**: This document object model grants access and modification of all document content and is standardized by the World Wide Web Consortium (W3C). This model is supported by almost all modern browsers today.

6.2 The IE4 DOM

The IE$ DOM was presented in Version 4 of Microsoft's Internet Explorer program. IE 5 and later forms incorporate help for most fundamental W3C DOM highlights.

6.2a Properties of the IE4 DOM

1. activeElement : It is a perused just property that alludes to the info component that is right now dynamic or being used (i.e., it has the information center).

2. Children[]:This is a cluster containing the HTML components that are the immediate offspring of the archive. Note this is not the same as the all [ ] cluster that contains every one of the components in the report, notwithstanding their particular situation in the control chain of command.

3. defaultCharset: this is simply the default character set of the report itself.

4. Expand: This property whenever set to forestalls customer side items from being extended therefore.

5. parenetWindow: This is the window that is containing the particular report.

6. readyState: This indicates the stacking status of an archive. It incorporates one of the accompanying four strings esteems: document.readystate

7. Uninitialized: This implies the archive has not begun stacking.

8. Loading: This implies the archive is stacking.

9. Interactive: This implies the archive has stacked adequately for the client to interface with it.

10. Complete: This implies finnthe archive is totally stacked.

6.3 Documents Methods in IE4DOM

IE4 DOM bolsters every one of the techniques accessible in the heritage DOM (Document Object Model).

1. clear() : Deprecated – Is the one in charge of deleting every one of the substances of the record and returns nothing by any stretch of the imagination.

2. close( ) : This is the one that shuts a report stream opened with the open( ) strategy and returns nothing by any stretch of the imagination.

3. open( ) : This is the one in charge of erases existing record substance and opens a stream through which new report substance might be composed thus and furthermore returns nothing by any stretch of the imagination.

4. write( ) : This is the one that embeds the predefined string or strings into the archive being parsed and annexes to reports opened with open( ). Returns nothing.

5. writeln( ) : This one is said to be indistinguishable from compose( ), with the exception of that it adds a newline character to the yield. Return.

Here is a guide to access archive properties utilizing IE4 DOM utilizing the chain of command and properties given above.

We can get to the principal structure component using document.forms[0].elements[0], etc.

```html
<html>
<head>
<title> Document Title </title>
<script type="text/javascript">
<!--
function myFunc(){
var ret = document.title;
alert("Document Title : " + ret );
var ret = document.URL;
alert("Document URL : " + ret );
var ret = document.forms[0];
alert("Document First Form : " + ret );
var ret = document.forms[0].elements[1];
alert("Second element : " + ret );
}
//-->
</script>
</head>
<body>
<h1 id="title">This is main title</h1>
<p>Click the following to see the result:</p>
<form name="FirstForm">
<input type="button" value="Click Me" onclick="myFunc();" />
<input type="button" value="Cancel">
</form>
<form name="SecondForm">
```

```
<input type="button" value="Don't ClickMe"/>

</form>

</body>

</html>
```

It is exceptionally fundamental to take note of that this model returns objects for structures and components and you would need to get to their qualities essentially by utilizing those item properties which are not talked about in this particular instructional exercise.

6.4 The Legacy DOM (Document Object Model)

This model was first presented in the prior renditions of the JavaScript Language. It is in this way upheld by all programs however awards get to just to a certain key segment of records for example, structures and pictures as it were. This model additionally gives numerous read-just properties, for example, title, URL, andlastModified that give data about the record all in all. Besides that, there are different strategies given by this model could be utilized to set and get archive property estimations too.

6.4a Properties in Legacy DOM

> ➤ alinkColor: This is portrayed as a string that determines the shade of initiated joins.

> ➤ anchors[ ] : This is can be depicted as a variety of Anchor objects, one for each stay that shows up in the predetermined archive.

➤ bgColor : This is a string wherein the foundation shade of the archive is determined.

➤ treat: This is a string esteemed property with unique conduct that guarantees the treats related to this record to be questioned and set.

➤ Area : This is a string that indicates the Internet space the record is from. It is significantly utilized for security reasons.

➤ embeds[ ] : This is characterized as a variety of articles that speak to the information implanted in the archive with the <embed> tag. An equivalent word for modules []. Some modules and ActiveX controls can be controlled with the JavaScript code.

➤ fgColor : This is a string that exclusively indicates the default content shading for which the record gave.

➤ forms[ ] : This is portrayed as a variety of Form objects, one for every HTML structure that shows up in the predetermined record.

➤ images [ ] : This is depicted as a variety of Image objects, one for each picture, that is implanted in the archive with the HTML <img> tag.

➤ lastModified: This is a perused just string that indicates the date of the latest change to the given report.

➤ linkColor: This is a string determining the shade of unvisited joins.

➢ Links[ ] : This is characterized as a report connection exhibit.

➢ Location: This is characterized as the URL of the record and it is deplored for the URL property.

➢ Plugins[ ] : This is an equivalent word for the embeds[ ].

➢ Referrer: This is characterized as a read-just string that contains the URL of the record, whenever gave, from which the present archive was connected.

➢ Title: This is depicted as the content substance of the <title> tag

➢ Url: This is portrayed as a read-just string that exclusively indicates the url of the particular record being referred to.

➢ vlinkColor: This is depicted as a string that explicitly picks the shade of visited joins.

6.5 Documents Methods in Legacy DOM (Document Object Model)

Explicit strategies that are upheld by the inheritance DOM is a similar route as the IE4 DOM given beforehand. These different strategies include:

1. clear() : Deprecated – This is the one that deletes the substance of a predefined archive and returns nothing by any stretch of the imagination.

2. close( ) : This is in charge of shutting a particular archive stream that was opened by the open( ) strategy and returns nothing by any stretch of the imagination.

3. open( ) : This is the one in charge of erasing existing archive substance and opening streams to which new report substance might be composed and comparatively return in nothing by any means.

4. write( ) : This is in charge of embeddings the predefined string or strings into the archive as of now being parsed or affixes to record opened with open( ). Returns nothing.

5. writeln( ) : This is indistinguishable from compose( ), aside from that it annexes a newline character to the yield and returns nothing by any means.

It is basic to take note of that you could find any HTML component inside any HTML archive utilizing HTML DOM. For example, in the event that a web report contains a structure component, at that point by utilizing JavaScript, we can allude to it as document.forms[0].

On the off chance that your Web report incorporates two structure components, the main structure is alluded to as document.forms[0] while the second is alluded to as document.forms[1].

Utilizing the different progressive systems and properties as talked about above, it is conceivable to get to the principal structure component utilizing document.forms[0].elements[0], etc. A case of this is given beneath:

```html
<html>
<head>
<title> Document Title </title>
<script type="text/javascript">
<!--
function myFunc()
{
var ret = document.title;
alert("Document Title : " + ret );
var ret = document.URL;
alert("Document URL : " + ret );

var ret = document.forms[0];
alert("Document First Form : " + ret );
var ret = document.forms[0].elements[1];
alert("Second element : " + ret );
}
//-->
</script>
</head>
<body>
<h1 id="title">This is main title</h1>
<p>Click the following to see the result:</p>
<form name="FirstForm">
<input type="button" value="Click Me" onclick="myFunc();" />
<input type="button" value="Cancel">
</form>
<form name="SecondForm">
<input type="button" value="Don't ClickMe"/>
</form>
</body>
</html>
```

The model above plainly outlines returns objects for structures and components and we would need to get to their qualities utilizing these item properties that are not examined in this particular instructional exercise.

6.6 The W3C DOM (Document Object Model)

In full, World Wide Consortium . This module institutionalizes the vast majority of the highlights of the inheritance DOM (Document Object Model) and includes new ones too. Besides the support of forms [ ], images[ ], and other cluster properties of the Document object, it additionally characterizes techniques that license contents to get to and control any report component however not simply unique reason components like structures and pictures.

6.7 Document Properties in W3C DOM

These backings every one of the properties accessible in Legacy DOM and they includes:

- ➤ alinkColor: This is characterized as the string that indicates the shade of initiated joins.

- ➤ anchors[ ] : This is characterized as a variety of Anchor objects, one for each stay which shows up in the report.

- ➤ bgColor : This is characterized as a string in charge of indicating the foundation shade of the particular report.

- ➤ treat: This is depicted as a string esteemed property that has uncommon conduct that permits the treats related to this particular record to be questioned and set.

➢ Area : This is characterized as a string that indicates the Internet space from which the archive is from. It is normally utilized for security purposes.

➢ embeds[ ] : This is characterized as a variety of items that speak to information inserted in a record with the <embed> tag. An equivalent word for modules []. Some modules and ActiveX controls can be constrained by JavaScript code.

➢ fgColor : This is a string that is in charge of determining the default content shading for the archive

➢ forms[ ] : This is characterized as a variety of Form objects, one for every HTML structure that shows up in a particular archive.

➤ images [ ] : It is just portrayed as a variety of Image objects, one for each picture that is inserted in a particular record with the HTML <img> tag.

➤ lastModified: This is portrayed as a read-just string that just determines the date of the latest change to the particular archive.

➤ linkColor: This is portrayed as a string that determines the shade of unvisited joins.

➤ Links[ ] : This is characterized as a report connection exhibit.

➤ Location: This is depicted as the URL of the archive. It typically expostulates for the URL property.

➤ Plugins[ ] : This is depicted as an equivalent word for the embeds[ ].

➢ Referrer: this is portrayed as a read-just string that has the URL of the archive, assuming any, from which the present record was connected earlier.

➢ Title: This is characterized as the content substance of the <title> tag

➢ Url: this is depicted as a read-just string that indicates the url of an archive.

➢ vlinkColor: This is a string that determines the shade of visited joins.

More properties that are added have to be identified as well and some of them include:

1. Body : This is a reference to the Element object that speaks to the <body> tag of this report.

2. defaultView : This is depicted as a read-just property that speaks to the window where a particular record is shown.

3. documentElement : This is portrayed as a read-just reference to the <html> tag of a record.

4. execution : This is portrayed as a read-just property that speaks to the DOM Implementation object which speaks to the usage that made this particular record.

6.8 Document Method in W3C DOM

This particular one bolsters every one of the techniques accessible in Legacy DOM. These techniques required are:

1. clear() : Deprecated. This is in charge of eradicating the substance of the report and returns nothing by any stretch of the imagination.

2. close( ) : This is depicted as the one that shuts a report stream that was opened with the open( ) technique and returns nothing.

3. open( ) : this is in charge of erasing sting report substance and opening a stream to which new archive substance could be composed. It additionally returns nothing by any means.

4. write( ) : this is portrayed as the one that is in charge of embeddings the predetermined string or strings into the particular record presently being parsed or annexes to report opened with open( ). It likewise returns nothing by any means.

5. writeln( ) : this is the one portrayed as the indistinguishable from compose( ), just that it affixss a newline character to the yield. It likewise returns nothing by any means.

There are additional lists of methods supported by W3C DOM. These methods include:

1. createeAttribute (name) : this is characterized as the one that profits a recently made Attr hub inside the predetermined name.

2. createComment(content) : this is the one that makes and returns another Comment hub containing the predefined content.

3. createDocumentFragment( ) : this is the one that makes and returns a vacant DocumentFragment hub.

4. createElement (tagName) : this characterized as one that makes and returns another Element hub with the predefined tag Name.

5. createTextNode(content): this is characterized as the one that makes and returns another Text hub that contains the predefined Text.

6. getElementById(id) : this is the one that profits the Element of this archive has the predefined esteem for its id property, or invalidates if no such Element exists in the record.

7. getElementsByName(name): this is depicted as one that profits a variety of hubs of all components in the record and has a predetermined incentive for their name quality. In the event that no such components are discovered, restores a zero-length exhibit.

8. getElementsByTagName(tagname): this is portrayed as the one that profits a variety of all Element hubs in this report have the predefined label name. The Element hubs show up in the returned exhibit in a similar request as they show up in the report source.

9. importNode(importedNode, profound): this is characterized as the one that is in charge of making and restoring a duplicate of a hub from some other record that is reasonable for inclusion into this archive. In the event that the profound contention is valid, it redundantly duplicates the offspring of the hub also. It is bolstered in DOMVersion2

Here is a given guide to access archive properties utilizing W3C DOM this strategy explicitly.

```
<html>
<head>
<title> Document Title </title>
<script type="text/javascript">
<!--
function myFunc()
{
var ret = document.getElementsByTagName("title");
alert("Document Title : " + ret[0].text );
var ret = document.getElementById("heading");
alert("Document URL : " + ret.innerHTML );
}
//-->
</script>
</head>
<body>
<h1 id="heading">This is main title</h1>
<p>Click the following to see the result:</p>
<form id="form1" name="FirstForm">
<input type="button" value="Click Me" onclick="myFunc();" />
<input type="button" value="Cancel">
</form>
<form d="form2" name="SecondForm">
<input type="button" value="Don't ClickMe"/>
</form>
</body>
</html>
```

It is exceptionally basic to take note of that this model is returning articles for structures and components and we would need to get to its qualities by utilizing those item properties that are not talked about in this particular instructional exercise.

6.9 The Standard

Utilizing obscure numeric codes in speaking to hub types is certainly not a very JavaScript like activity by any means. In another section there will be observation on the pieces that are different for the interface of the DOM which may be seen as outsider. It is worth noting that the DOM was meant for more uses than just on JavaScript. Still maybe it aims for more purpose which can be put to use in frameworks that differe as well as use in HTML and XML as well.

This is extremely heartbreaking. Models are typically helpful. In any case, for this situation, the preferred position (cross-language consistency) isn't too persuading. When you have an interface that is input with the language you are using it will save you time.

For instance of this poor incorporation, consider the childNodes property that component hubs in the DOM have. This property more often than not holds a cluster like an item, with a length property and properties marked by numbers to get to the kid hubs.

This is an occurrence of the NodeList type, not a genuine exhibit, therefore it doesn't have strategies, for example, cut and guide to be accurate.

At that point there are issues that are basically inadequately structured in nature. For instance, there is no real way to make another hub at all and afterward promptly add kids or ascribes to it because of the new creation.

Or maybe, you need to initially make it until you've completed and after that include the youngsters or traits each in turn, utilizing reactions also. Codes that connect vigorously with the DOM will in general get long, redundant and monstrous which is obviously exceptionally dreary and depleting.

Anyway these imperfections are not lethal by any means. Since JavaScript awards clients an opportunity to make their own reflections, it is conceivable to configuration improved methods for communicating the activities you are performing to meet your ideal targets. Various libraries expected for program programming accompany such devices joined to them.

6.10 Finding Elements

Exploring these connections among guardians, kids, and kin is typically helpful. Rather, in the event that you need to locate a particular hub in a report, arriving at it by beginning at the document body and following a fixed way of properties is an impractical notion. By doing so you heating suspicions into your program about the exact structure of the current archive—a structure you might need to change later on as your needs change. The way that content hubs are made notwithstanding for the whitespace between hubs is another convoluting factor.

The model report's <body> tag doesn't have only three kids (<h1> and two <p> components) yet rather has seven: those three, or more the spaces previously, after, and between them.

Along these lines in the event that you need to get the href quality of the connection in that archive, you wouldn't have any desire to state something like "Get the subsequent kid or the 6th offspring of the record's body". Rather it'd be better on the off chance that you could state "Get the main connection in the archive". Also, sure you could.

```
let link = document.body.getElementsByTagName("a")[0];
console.log(link.href);
```

All component hubs have a getElementsByTagName strategy, that gathers all components with the given label name that are relatives (legitimately or in a roundabout way) of that hub and returns them as a cluster like an article. To locate a particular single hub, you could select to give it an id characteristic and use document.getElementById.

```
<p>My ostrich Gertrude:</p>
<p><img id="gertrude" src="img/ostrich.png"></p>
<script>
let ostrich = document.getElementById("gertrude");
console.log(ostrich.src);
</script>
```

A third method is getElementsByClassName, which, like getElementsByTagName, searches through the contents of an element node retrieving all elements that have the given string in their class attribute.

6.11 Creating the Nodes

In a perfect world nearly everything about the DOM information structure can be modified. The state of the archive tree can be adjusted by changing the parent-kid connections. Hubs have an expel technique that expels them from their present parent hub completely.

So as to add a kid hub to a component hub, you can utilize appendChild, which puts it toward the finish of the rundown of youngsters, or insertBefore, which embeds the hub given as the main contention before the hub allowed as the subsequent contention.

```
<p>One</p>
<p>Two</p>
<p>Three</p>
<script>
let paragraphs = document.body.getElementsByTagName("p");
document.body.insertBefore(paragraphs[2], paragraphs[0]);
</script>
```

A hub could likewise exist in a report in just one spot. In this way, embeddings passage Three before section One will from the start expel it from the finish of the record and afterward embed it at the front, bringing about Three/One/Two.

Every one of the tasks that addition a hub some place will, in the long run, cause it to be expelled from its present position (on the off chance that it has one).

The replaceChild strategy is utilized to supplant a kid hub with another. It takes as contentions two hubs: another hub and the hub to be supplanted. The supplanted hub ought to be an offspring of the component the technique has approached. Note that both replaceChild and insertBefore anticipate the new hub as their first contentions.

Let's assume you need to compose a content that replaces all pictures (<img> labels) in a record with a book held in their alt traits, which indicates an option printed portrayal of the picture. This procedure includes expelling the pictures as well as adding another content hub to supplant them. Content hubs are made by the document.createTextNode technique.

```
<p>The <img src="img/cat.png" alt="Cat"> in the
<img src="img/hat.png" alt="Hat">.</p>
<p><button onclick="replaceImages()">Replace</button></p>
<script>
function replaceImages() {
let images = document.body.getElementsByTagName("img");
for (let i = images.length - 1; i >= 0; i--) {
let image = images[i];
if (image.alt) {
let text = document.createTextNode(image.alt);
image.parentNode.replaceChild(text, image);


}
}
}
</script>
```

Given a string, createTextNode gives you a book hub that you could embed into an archive to make it appear on the screen. The circle that goes over the pictures begins toward the finish of the rundown.

This is fundamental in light of the fact that the hub rundown returned by a technique like getElementsByTagName (or on the other hand a property like childNodes) is live. That is, it is refreshed as the record changes.

On the off chance that you began from the front, expelling the primary picture would make the rundown lose its first component in this manner the second time the circle rehashes, where I am 1, it would stop on the grounds that the length of the accumulation is presently additionally 1.

In the event that you need a strong accumulation of hubs, rather than a live one, you could change over the gathering to a genuine cluster just by calling Array.from.

```
let arrayish = {0: "one", 1: "two", length: 2};
let array = Array.from(arrayish);
console.log(array.map(s => s.toUpperCase()));
```

To make component hubs, you could utilize the document.createElement technique. This strategy takes a label name and returns another unfilled hub of the given kind. For example, the model underneath characterizes a utility, which makes a component hub and treats the remainder of its contentions as offspring of that hub.

This capacity is then used to add an ascribed to a statement.

```
<blockquote id="quote">
No book can ever be finished. While working on it we learn
just enough to find it immature the moment we turn away
from it.
</blockquote>

<script>
function elt(type, ...children) {
let node = document.createElement(type);
for (let child of children) {
if (typeof child != "string") node.appendChild(child);
else node.appendChild(document.createTextNode(child));
}
return node;



}
document.getElementById("quote").appendChild(
elt("footer", "—",
elt("strong", "Karl Popper"),
", preface to the second edition of ",

elt("em", "The Open Society and Its Enemies"),
", 1950")));
</script>
```

6.12 General Attributes

Other component traits, for example, href for connections, can be gotten through a property of a similar name as the component's DOM object. For most ordinarily utilized standard properties this is the situation.

Nonetheless, HTML awards you an opportunity to set any trait you need on hubs. This could be valuable since it enables you to store additional data in a given report. On the off chance that you concoct your own characteristic names, such traits won't be available as properties on the component's hub. Or maybe, you would need to utilize the getAttribute and setAttribute techniques to work with them.

```
<p data-classified="secret">The launch code is 00000000.</p>
<p data-classified="unclassified">I have two feet.</p>
<script>
let paras = document.body.getElementsByTagName("p");
for (let para of Array.from(paras)) {
if (para.getAttribute("data-classified") == "secret") {
para.remove();
}
}
</script>
```

It is instructed to prefix the names regarding such made-up characteristics with information so they don't strife with different qualities. There is a generally utilized quality, class, which is a catchphrase in the JavaScript language.

For verifiable reasons—some old JavaScript executions were not ready to deal with property names that coordinated catchphrases—the property used to get to this quality is called className. You could likewise get to it under its actual name, "class", by utilizing the getAttribute and setAttribute strategies.

6.13 DOM Styling

We have seen that distinctive HTML components are drawn in an unexpected way. Some are shown as squares and others inline. Some include styling— <strong> making its substance strong, and <a> making it blue and underlining it.

The way a <img> label demonstrates a picture or a <a> label makes a connection be pursued when it is clicked, is unequivocally attached to the component type. Anyway you could change the styling related to the component, for example, the content shading or underline. This is a model that uses the style property:

```
<p><a href=".">Normal link</a></p>
<p><a href="." style="color: green">Green link</a></p>
```

The subsequent connection will be green rather than the default connection shading. A style quality could contain more than one announcement, which is a property, (for example, shading) trailed by a colon and a worth, (for example, green).

In the event that there is more than one announcement, it must be isolated by semicolons, as in

"color: red; border: none".

A lot of aspects of the document could be influenced by styling. For instance, the display property controls whether an element is displayed as a block or as an inline element.

This text is displayed \inline\,
\as a block\, and
\not at all

The square label will wind up without anyone else line since square components are not shown in accordance with the writings around them. The last tag isn't shown in any way—show: none keeps a component from appearing on the screen.

This is a decent method to shroud components. It is typically desirable to expel them from the archive since it makes it simpler to uncover them again later.

JavaScript code could control the style of a component through the component's style property legitimately. This property holds an article that has properties for all conceivable style properties. The estimations of these properties are strings, since we could compose along these lines changing a specific part of the component's style.

```
<p id="para" style="color: purple">
Nice text
</p>
<script>

let para = document.getElementById("para");
console.log(para.style.color);
para.style.color = "magenta";
</script>
```

Some style property names have hyphens, for example, textual style family. Given that such property names are cumbersome to work with in JavaScript (you'd need to state style["font-family"]), the property names in the style object for such properties have their very own hyphens expelled and the letters after then promoted (style.fontFamily).

6.14 Cascading Styles

The styling system for HTML is called CSS, for Cascading Style Sheets. A stylesheet is a set of rules to govern how to style elements in a document. It could be given inside a <style> tag.

```
strong {
font-style: italic;
color: gray;
}
</style>

<p>Now <strong>strong text</strong> is italic and gray.</p>
```

The falling in the name just alludes to the way that few such guidelines are consolidated together to create the last style for a component. In the model, the default styling for <strong> labels, which gives them text style weight: striking, is overlaid by the standard in the <style> tag, which includes textual style and shading.

At the point when a few principles are applied to characterize an incentive for a similar property, the most as of late read standard gets a higher priority and along these lines it wins.

On the off chance that the standard in the <style> label included textual style weight: typical, repudiating the default textual style weight rule, the content would be ordinary, not strong. Style is a style ascribe applied straightforwardly to the hubs that have the most noteworthy priority and consistently win.

It is really conceivable to target things other than label names in CSS rules. A standard for .abc applies to all components with "abc" in their group property. A standard for #xyz applies to the component with an id property of "xyz" (which ought to be remarkable inside the doled out archive).

```
.subtle {
color: gray;
font-size: 80%;
}
#header {
background: blue;
color: white;
}
/* p elements with id main and with classes a and b */
p#main.a.b {
margin-bottom: 20px;
}
```

The priority guideline supporting the most as of late characterized standard applies just if the principles have a similar particularity.

This is a proportion of how definitely it depicts coordinating components, controlled by the number and kind (tag, class, or ID) of component angles it requires. For example, a standard that objectives p.a is more explicit than guidelines that target p or only .an and would in this manner overshadow them.

The documentation p > a ... {} applies the offered styles to all <a> labels that are immediate offspring of <p> labels. So also, p a ... {} applies to all <a> labels inside <p> labels, regardless of whether they are immediate or aberrant kids.

6.15 Query Selectors

You won't utilize templates such a great amount in this book as might be normal. Understanding them is basic when programming in the program however they are entangled enough to warrant a different book all together for you to cover them well.

The fundamental motivation behind why a client is acquainted with selector linguistic structure, which is the documentation utilized in templates to figure out which components a lot of styles apply to, is that you could utilize this equivalent smaller than normal language as a successful method to discover DOM components.

The querySelectorAll technique, is characterized both on the archive object and on component hubs, takes a selector string and returns a NodeList containing every one of the components that it matches.

```html
<p>And if you go chasing
<span class="animal">rabbits</span></p>
<p>And you know you're going to fall</p>
<p>Tell 'em a <span class="character">hookah smoking
<span class="animal">caterpillar</span></span></p>
<p>Has given you the call</p>
<script>
function count(selector) {
return document.querySelectorAll(selector).length;
}
console.log(count("p")); // All <p> elements
// → 4
console.log(count(".animal")); // Class animal
// → 2
console.log(count("p .animal")); // Animal inside of <p>
// → 2
console.log(count("p > .animal")); // Direct child of <p>
// → 1
</script>
```

Not at all like strategies, for example, getElementsByTagName, the item returned by querySelectorAll is said to be not live. It won't change in the event that you changed the record. It is as yet not a genuine cluster. Nonetheless, regardless you have to call Array.from in the event that you need to treat it like one.

The querySelector strategy (without the All part) works along these lines also. This is helpful in the event that you need a particular, single component. It will possibly return if the primary coordinating component or invalid when no component matches.

6.16 DOM Summary

There is a need for all projects of JavaScript to go through a reviewing process as well as be able to meddle with an archive that is the one being shown through a structure of the information which is what is called the DOM. This structure is mostly known for its ability to communicate with the models of the various programs that are the ones to be recorded and a program of JavaScript is the one to be adjusted in order to make changes in how the whole report will eventually be perceived. JavaScript projects may review and meddle with an archive that the program is showing through an information structure called the DOM (Document Object Model). This structure speaks to the program's model of the record, and a JavaScript program could adjust it to change the percievability of the report as required.

It is only the DOM that is framed in a manner that is similar to that of how a tree is shaped in the first place.

The goal which is at the edge of each and every component is that which are placed in a dominant position in order to move on with great progress according to how it is framed as well as how it will be noted down at the very end. The DOM (Document Object Model) is sorted out like a tree, with the end goal that components are masterminded progressively as per the structure of the particular record. The articles that speak to components have properties, for example, parentNode and childNodes, which could be utilized to explore through this tree.

The manner in which an archive is shown could be affected by either styling, both by joining styles to hubs legitimately or by characterizing decides that could coordinate certain hubs. There are a lot of various style properties, for example, shading or show. JavaScript code could control a component's style straightforwardly through its style property. There is a specified way through which the information that is archived is said to be affected either in how it is styled in which case they can make use of styles for joining both together.

Chapter 7: JavaScript Cookies

There would be no JavaScript at all without internet browsers. Be that as it may, regardless of whether there were, nobody would have given any consideration to them. Decentralization of web innovation has been available from the beginning, in fact as well as in the manner in which it has advanced all through time. A few program sellers have included new functionalities in specially appointed and now and then ill-conceived ways, which wound up being embraced by others lastly set down as in norms.

This is both a gift and a revile. On the one hand, it is fundamental to not host a focal gathering control a framework and have it be improved by different gatherings working in free coordinated effort (or periodically open threatening vibe). Then again, the heedless manner by which the Web was created implies that the subsequent framework is certainly not a brilliant illustration of inside consistency by any stretch of the imagination. Portions of it are out and out befuddling and misguided.

The World Wide Web (not to be mistaken for the Internet all in all) is a lot of conventions and configurations that award us opportunities to visit website pages in a program. The "Internet" some portion of the name alludes to the pages that can without much of a stretch connect to one another, along these lines associating into a colossal work that clients can travel through. Http is a stateless convention. It is important to keep up session data between various pages. The most proficient strategy for recollecting and following buys is utilizing treats.

One sends information to the program as a treat. The program could then acknowledge the treat. On the off chance that it does, it is put away as a plain book record on the guest's hard drive. Accordingly, when the guest lands on another page on their site, the program sends a similar treat to the server for recovery. After recovery, the server knows/recalls what it was that was put away before.

7.1 Components of cookies

Expires: This is the date the treat will lapse. In the event that it is clear, the treat will terminate when the guest stops the program.

- Domain: The area name of your site.

- Path: Is the way to the catalog or site page that set the treat. This could be clear in the event that you need to recover the treat from any registry or page.

- Secure: If this field contains "secure", the treat may just be recovered with a protected server. In the event that the field is clear, no such confinements exist.

- Name=Value: Cookies are set and recovered as key-esteem sets.

Initially treats were intended for CGI programming. The information contained in a treat is consequently transmitted to the internet browser and the web server. Consequently CGI contents on the server could be perused and compose treat esteems that are put away on the customer.

7.2 Types of Cookies

7.2a Technical Cookies

Specialized treats are utilized for the sole motivation behind "completing the transmission of a correspondence over an electronic interchange arrange and are as carefully important for the supplier as a Company data administration expressly mentioned by the endorser or the client to give this administration. They don't have different purposes and are regularly introduced by the proprietor or administrator of the site.

They significantly permit the ordinary route and utilization of the site (permitting, for instance, to complete a buy or validation for access to confined territories). They are in actuality important for the correct activities of the site just as those that empower you to peruse dependent on a progression of chose criteria (for example, language chose items to buy) so as to improve the administration.

Earlier client's assent isn't required for the establishment of these treats.

7.2b Profiling Cookies

These treats are planned for making profiles identified with you and are utilized to send promoting messages in accordance with the inclinations that appeared by a similar part while surfing the net. On account of outsider treats, the site doesn't have an immediate command over individual treats and can't control them (it can't introduce them legitimately nor erase them). You could in any case, deal with these treats through the program settings (adhere to the guidelines underneath), or locales recorded in "Oversee Cookies".

For the utilization of profiling treats, assent is required. In like manner, the client could approve or preclude the assent from claiming the establishment of treats through the alternatives in "Oversee Cookies".

7.2c Session Cookies

These are transitory treats that terminate toward the finish of a program session. That is, the point at which you leave the site.

Session treats enable the site to remember you as you explore through pages during a solitary program session and enable you to utilize the site all the more effectively. For example, session treats empower a site to recall that a client has put things in a web based shopping bin.

7.2d Persistent Cookies

Tireless treats are put away on your gear between perusing sessions until expiry or erasure. This is rather than session treats. In this manner they empower the site to "remember" you on your arrival, recall your inclinations and tailor administrations for you.

What's more, there might be different treats which are set by the site which you have visited, for example, this site, so as to furnish you or outsiders with data.

Most programs are at first set to acknowledge treats. Be that as it may, you can debilitate treats as you wish. For the most part this could be through changing your web programming perusing settings. It is additionally conceivable to arrange your program settings to empower acknowledgment of explicit treats or to inform you each time another treat is going to be put away on your PC. In this manner empowering you to choose whether to acknowledge or dismiss the treat. So as to deal with your utilization of treats there are different assets available to you, for example the "Help" segment on your program could help you. You could likewise impair or erase the put away information utilized by innovation like treats, for example, Local Shared Objects or Flash treats, by dealing with your program's "add-on settings" or by essentially visiting the site of its supplier.

Given our treats enable you to get to a portion of your site's basic highlights, I suggest that you leave treats empowered. In the event that treats are handicapped, it could imply that you would experience diminished usefulness or could be kept from utilizing that site by and large.

7.3 Storing Cookies

Both http solicitation and reaction messages could contain headers. Solicitation headers could incorporate favored language, client operator or acknowledged encoding. Reaction headers ordinarily contain properties, for example, reserving orders, content sort and language.

In the event that the server needs to put a treat, it sets the Set-Cookie header with the treat's substance. For example, Wikipedia places a treat with your assessed physical area.

Set-Cookie: GeoIP=NL:Nijmegen:51.8333:5.8667:v4; Domain=.wikipedia.org

The Domain catchphrase species for which the web area, the treat will be connected to the solicitation. The situation of treats can't be ensured; customer approach may direct to disregard it.

On the off chance that the customer spared the treat, it would send the Cookie header to every single resulting demand in the solicitation header.

Cookie: GeoIP=NL:Nijmegen:51.8333:5.8667:v4;

Cookies can also be stored and retrieved by the client with JavaScript.

```
document.cookie="GeoIP=NL:Nijmegen:51.8333:5.8667:v4;
Domain=.wikipedia.org";
```

At sight, the probability of putting away and recovering treats on the customer side appears to incredibly expand conceivable outcomes. Anyway this is just mostly obvious. Putting away and recovering treats can undoubtedly be duplicated by introducing http demands with JavaScript. Sparing treats would be equivalent to making a solicitation with the favored treat information as solicitation contention.

A web server utilizing that contention in the Set-Cookie header of the reaction would put it in the program. Perusing treats would be equivalent to mentioning a page which restored the treat information that was sent in the solicitation header. Moreover, when utilizing JavaScript, the genuine treat stockpiling is similarly as unsure on the grounds that it likewise relies upon the treat approach of the customer.

Be that as it may, a similar articulation power would possibly be accomplished if the server executes this sort of copying. Practically speaking, sparing and perusing treats with JavaScript opens up new conceivable outcomes just as dangers. These dangers could include treat robbery which could prompt session commandeering. At the point when outsider's JavaScript is incorporated into a page, the immediate access to treats empowers the assailant to move treats to his own space.

7.4 Same-origin policy

What treats to be put away and recovered for every space is managed by the equivalent source strategy. This website architecture rule expresses that data put away in the program by one area could later be perused just or adjusted by a similar space. By actualizing this strategy, sites can gently exist together on a program with one another without meddling. This strategy goes back to adaptation 2 of the Netscape program.

The equivalent birthplace approach adequately confines treats. This makes them just available to the site putting away them. The Domain watchword we found in Wikipedia treat accordingly just influences whether the treat information is imparted to its sub spaces and it can never be imparted to different areas. A similar standard applies when putting away and recovering treats with JavaScript.

In spite of the fact that the equivalent starting point approach has been around for quite a while, no program completely actualizes it for all perusing data.

Inability to do so is one reason why web information spills. Anyway all programs uphold an equivalent starting point strategy for treat information.

The most straightforward approach to make a treat is to appoint a string an incentive to the document.cookie object, which is represented underneath

```
document.cookie = "key1=value1;key2=value2;expires=date";
```

Treat esteems may exclude semicolons, commas, or whitespace. Henceforth, you might need to utilize the JavaScript escape() capacity to encode the incentive before putting away it in the treat.

By doing this, you would likewise need to utilize the comparing unescape() work when you read the treat esteem.

```html
<html>
<head>
<script type="text/javascript">
<!--
function WriteCookie()
{
if( document.myform.customer.value == "" ){
alert ("Enter some value!");
return;
}
cookievalue= escape(document.myform.customer.value) + ";";
document.cookie="name=" + cookievalue;
document.write ("Setting Cookies : " + "name=" + cookievalue );
}
//-->
</script>
</head>
<body>
<form name="myform" action="">
Enter name: <input type="text" name="customer"/>
<input type="button" value="Set Cookie" onclick="WriteCookie();"/>
</form>
</body>
</html>
```

7.5 Reading Cookies

This is essentially similar to composing a treat. The document.cookie string will keep a rundown of name=value sets isolated by semicolons, where name is the name of a treat and worth is its string esteem.

```
<html>
<head>
<script type="text/javascript">
<!--
function ReadCookie()
{
var allcookies = document.cookie;
document.write ("All Cookies : " + allcookies );
// Get all the cookies pairs in an array
cookiearray = allcookies.split(';');
// Now take key value pair out of this array
for(var i=0; i<cookiearray.length; i++){
name = cookiearray[i].split('=')[0];
value = cookiearray[i].split('=')[1];
document.write ("Key is : " + name + " and Value is : " + value);
}
}
//-->
</script>
</head>
<body>
<form name="myform" action="">
<p> click the following button and see the result:</p>
<input type="button" value="Get Cookie" onclick="ReadCookie()"/>
</form>
</body>
</html>
```

Length is a strategy for Array class which returns the length of an exhibit.

We will talk about Arrays in a different part. By that point, it would be ideal if you attempt to process it.

One will speculate that following by an outsider is beyond the realm of imagination if an equivalent beginning arrangement is authorized, since it squares moving identifiers to an outsider. This was to be sure the situation for more established treat norms, which determined that sharing of treats between servers ought to be restricted yet with more current measures this prerequisite was loose .Although treats can at present just be put away and recovered alone space, implanted outer components, for example, pictures or casings permit treats collaboration on their (outsider) area. Treats set during the recovery of outside components are called outsider treats. At the point when treats are utilized to follow a client, they are as often as possible named 'following treats'.

How at that point do outsider treats work? The site proprietor implants a bit of outer substance on his web to show notices or empowering informal communities or web investigation. At the point when a page is stacked, so are the outsider components.

Treats set by these components must be perused by their own space, however since similar outsiders are incorporated on various sites, each site adds to the profile of the guest. This profile is stretched out with data that is accessible to the outsider, for example, the location of the website page it was inserted on.

There are two regular methods that make outsiders treat following increasingly successful. In the first place, some website page properties, for example, page title, can be mentioned by the outsider's casing in light of the fact that their properties are shared.

In this manner these properties ought not to contain recognizable data. Studies have discovered that the greater part of the sites researched straightforwardly released private data, for example, names and addresses and even spilled properties like client IDs. Also, some outsiders require installing contents legitimately into the principal gathering's site. The outsider at that point turns into a first gathering in this way empowering procedures like treat synchronization between the first and the outsider. Outsider treat arrangement can be sidestepped since the outsider goes about as a first gathering.

Most work area browsers1 give alternatives to control treat arrangement, for example, obstructing all treats or treats starting from outsiders.

Choices are anyway accessible to expel treats when the bowser is shut. Moreover, most programs take into account tuning the treat approach on a for each site premise. Program augmentations are accessible to disentangle this procedure. Versatile browsers2 have fundamentally little choices accessible and need module capacities.

On Safari, outsider treats are hindered as a matter of course. An outsider treat isn't blocked when at any rate one treat on the objective area has been put away previously. This adequately squares outsider treats just when the outsider has not been visited as a first gathering. Mozilla pondered blocking outsider treats naturally, however deferred execution in light of the fact that further research was required. The meaning of 'blocking' contrasts from program to program. For example, Internet Explorer just hinders the capacity of an outsider treat, though Firefox squares perusing the treat. A perfect outsider blocking framework would deny both perusing and composing.

7.6 Deleting a Cookie

Here and there you will need to erase a treat so ensuing endeavors to peruse the treat return nothing. You simply need to set the expiry date to a period in the past to accomplish this.

For instance:

```
<html>
<head>
<script type="text/javascript">
<!--
function WriteCookie()
{
var now = new Date();
now.setMonth( now.getMonth() - 1 );
cookievalue = escape(document.myform.customer.value) + ";"
document.cookie="name=" + cookievalue;
document.cookie = "expires=" + now.toUTCString() + ";"
document.write("Setting Cookies : " + "name=" + cookievalue );
}
//-->
</script>
</head>
<body>
<form name="formname" action="">
Enter name: <input type="text" name="customer"/>
<input type="button" value="Set Cookie" onclick="WriteCookie()"/>
</form>
```

7.7 Summary

Numerous strategies are accessible to diligently store data in a program. Treats are to a great extent utilized for capacity, yet different systems have additionally risen. These procedures known as super treats are various strategies with various solid and frail focuses.

Reserve could as of now be utilized to tenaciously store one of a kind recognizable proof by means of super treat strategies dependent on headers. These techniques, in principle, could be effectively bypassed by modifying headers by means of intermediary or program augmentations. Because of the presentation of store treats, this is not true anymore. Reserve treats utilize a method to catch with the store and no simple arrangement appears to exist to forestall them.

Perusing the web without being followed is hard. This is a result of reserve treats and different techniques. The best way to anticipate all following strategies dependent on information stockpiling is to cripple reserve, history, treats and module stockpiling.

The cookiewet was acquainted with illuminate clients pretty much all non-vital treats. Its extension is appropriately characterized. The two treats and super treats appear to be influenced by it. This is on the grounds that the treat law just recognizes two kinds of treats and it is difficult to have an effect between various degrees of security encroachment. Institutionalized symbols could be utilized to improve client's understanding. Anyway the law doesn't shield clients from questionable following strategies, if only illuminates. New enactment must be proposed if assurance is considered a need.

Very little research has been finished concerning the super treats. A survey of all program perspectives and their relentless stockpiling probabilities could present more methods for perseveringly putting away data in a program. This data ought to be remembered when drafting new web determination. This is on the grounds that program merchants regularly need to adjust between following the web determinations and securing their clients' protection.

This issue could be dodged if protection results were a better idea during the formation of web particulars.

Besides, I would suggest benchmarking the mix of different super treat strategies. Testing them on an enormous and agent site should give you knowledge into how regularly clients clear their treats and what number of these clients can in any case be distinguished utilizing super treats.

It would likewise be fascinating to make a program planned for anticipating all known super treat strategies.

We have just observed that some super treat properties contact the center of perusing standards. Research would in this way need to indicate what sort of perusing knowledge remains when a few highlights are yielded so as to improve online security.

Chapter 8: Regular Expression

Programming apparatuses and methods endure and spread in a disorderly, developmental way. It's not generally the pretty or splendid ones that success. Or maybe the ones that capacity all around ok inside the correct specialty or that happen to be incorporated with another fruitful bit of innovation. In this section, I will talk about one such device, customary articulations.

Ordinary articulations are an approach to portray designs in string information. They structure a little, separate language that is a piece of the JavaScript and various different dialects and frameworks. Customary articulations are both frightfully ungainly and amazingly helpful. Their linguistic structure is enigmatic, and the programming interface JavaScript accommodates these articulations is ungainly. Anyway they are an integral asset for assessing and handling strings.

Appropriately understanding ordinary articulations could make you a viable software engineer.

The JavaScript RegExp class speaks to normal articulations, and both String and RegExp characterize techniques that utilization customary articulations to perform design coordinating and search-and-supplant works on content.

8.1 Creating a Regular Expression

A standard articulation is a sort of article that could be either built with the RegExp constructor or composed as a strict incentive by encasing an example in forwarding cut (/) characters.

let re1 = new RegExp("abc"); let re2 = /abc/;

Both of those standard articulation articles speak to a similar example: a character pursued by a b then by a c. When utilizing the RegExp constructor, the example is composed as a typical string therefore the standard guidelines apply for oblique punctuation lines. The subsequent documentation treats oblique punctuation lines to some degree all the more in an unexpected way. To begin with, since forward cut parts of the bargains, need to put an oblique punctuation line before any forward slice that you need to be a piece of the example. Also, oblique punctuation lines that aren't a piece of the exceptional character codes (like \n) will be protected, as opposed to disregard as they are in strings, and change the significance of the example. A few characters, for example, a question mark and an or more sign have extraordinary implications in ordinary articulations and along these lines must be gone before by an oblique punctuation line in the event that they are intended to speak to the character itself.

let eighteenPlus = /eighteen\+/;

Testing for matches Regular articulation items has various strategies. The easiest one is testing. On the off chance that you pass it a string, it will restore a Boolean revealing to you whether the string contains a match of the example in the articulation.

```
console.log(/abc/.test("abcde")); // → true
console.log(/abc/.test("abxde")); // → false
```

An ordinary articulation comprising of just nonspecial characters. These essentially speak to the succession of characters.

On the off chance that abc happens anyplace in the string you are trying against (not exactly toward the beginning), the test will return genuine.

Sets of characters seeing if a string contains 'abc' should too be possible with a call to indexOf. Normal articulations enable us to express progressively muddled examples. Let's assume you need to coordinate any number in a normal articulation, putting a lot of characters between square sections makes that piece of the articulation coordinate any of the characters between the sections. Both of the accompanying articulations coordinate all strings that contain a digit:

```
console.log(/[0123456789]/.test("in 1992")); // → true console.log(/[0-9]/.test("in 1992")); // → true
```

Inside square sections, a hyphen (-) between two characters could be utilized to show a scope of characters, where the requesting is dictated by the character's Unicode number. Characters 0 to 9 sit directly by one another in this requesting (codes 48 to 57), so [0-9] covers every one of them and matches all digits.

Various regular character gatherings have their own worked in alternate ways. Digits are among them: \d implies a similar thing as [0-9]. \d Any digit character \w An alphanumeric character ("word character") \s Any whitespace character (space, tab, newline, and comparable) \D A character that isn't a digit \W A no alphanumeric character \S A non-whitespace character .

Any character aside from newline could coordinate a date and time arrangement like 01-30-2003 15:20 with the accompanying articulation:

```
let dateTime = /\d\d-\d\d-\d\d\d\d \d\d:\d\d/;
console.log(dateTime.test("01-30-2003 15:20")); // → true
console.log(dateTime.test("30-jan-2003 15:20")); // → false
```

That looks totally horrendous. Half of it is oblique punctuation lines, delivering a foundation clamor that makes it difficult to recognize the real example communicated. You'll see a marginally improved variant of this articulation later. These oblique punctuation line codes could likewise be utilized inside square sections.

For instance, [\d.] implies any digit or a period character. Be that as it may, if the period itself loses its extraordinary importance. The equivalent goes for other uncommon characters, for example, +.

To reverse a lot of characters—that is, to express that you need to coordinate any character with the exception of the ones in the set—you can compose a caret (^) character after the opening section.

```
let notBinary = /[^01]/; console.log(notBinary.test("1100100010100110"));
// → false console.log(notBinary.test("1100100010200110")); // → true
```

Rehashing portions of an example we presently realize how to coordinate a solitary digit. Consider the possibility that you need to coordinate an entire number—a succession of at least one digits. When you put an or more sign (+) subsequent to something in a customary articulation, it implies that the component might be rehashed more than one time along these lines,/\d+/matches at least one digit characters.

```
console.log(/'\d+'/.test("'123'")); // → true console.log(/'\d+'/.test("'"')); //
→ false console.log(/'\d*'/.test("'123'")); // → true
console.log(/'\d*'/.test("'"')); // → true
```

The star (*) has a comparable significance yet in addition concedes the example an opportunity to match multiple times. Something with a star after it never keeps an example from coordinating. It'll simply match zero occasions on the off chance that it can't locate any appropriate content to coordinate.

A question mark makes a piece of an example discretionary also, which means it could happen multiple times or one time as required. In the model beneath, u character is permitted to happen, yet the example likewise coordinates when it is absent.

```
let neighbor = /neighbou?r/; console.log(neighbor.test("neighbour")); // →
true console.log(neighbor.test("neighbor")); // → true
```

Use props to show that an example ought to happen at a specified time in terms of numbers. Placing {4} to follow a component as a sample will require it to take place with at most precision numerous times.

It is likewise conceivable to determine a range along these lines: {2,4} implies the component must happen a negligible twice and at most extreme multiple times. Here is another form of the date and time design that permits both single and twofold digit days, months, and hours. It is likewise somewhat simpler to unravel.

```
let dateTime = /\d{1,2}-\d{1,2}-\d{4} \d{1,2}:\d{2}/;
console.log(dateTime.test("1-30-2003 8:45")); // → true
```

You could likewise indicate open-finished extents when utilizing props. This is accomplished by excluding the number after the comma. Therefore, {5,} implies at least multiple times.

Gathering sub articulations to utilize an administrator like * or + on more than each component in turn, you would need to utilize enclosures. A piece of a standard articulation that is encased in brackets considers a solitary component to the extent the administrator's tailing will be of any concern.

```
let cartoonCrying = /boo+(hoo+)+/i;
console.log(cartoonCrying.test("Boohoooohoohooo")); // → true
```

The + characters that appear as number one and two are said to be able to apply solely to the following o in hoo and also in boo but in a separate manner. The + which is number three is applied to all the gatherings while arranging at the very least a singular succession similar to it.

At the very end the I which is on the model is the one to make the articulation said to be customary be obtuse which will in turn allow it to arrange the B which is in capital form and inside the string info even though the sample given will be given in the lower case.

8.2 Match ()

It is said that gatherings and matches are the most on point approach in the coordination of an articulation which is standard. It is characterized by its ability to show you if it is well arranged or if it not well arranged at all. Articulations that are said to be ordinary have what is known as a technique of executive known to take back invalid when there is no match to be found anywhere and therefore the article is taken back with the info stating the general match.

```
let match = /\d+/.exec("one two 100"); console.log(match); // → ["100"]
console.log(match.index); // → 8
```

It is important to note that anything that returns from the executive contains a property record that clearly shows you the very position the match which is fruitfully initialized. It is also worth noting that there is a similarity to a number of strings with the match which is characterized by being the initial component coordinated by the string.

Recall the model a while back in which a similar type of digits grouping was what we were is a search of. Esteems of strings are said to contain a strategy of matching said to correspondingly carry on.

```
console.log("one two 100".match(/\d+/)); // → ["100"]
```

When the point comes for the articulation which is said to be ordinary is said to be containing articulations which are of a sub nature which are arranged within the enclosures, the material responsible for the gathering has to also be present within the enclosure as well.

The main component is said to be the match in its entire entirety. Below you will find a component that is arranged by the main gathering at the position of the gathering which is subsequent in nature as well:

```
let quotedText = /'([^']*)'/; console.log(quotedText.exec("she said 'hello'"));
// → ["'hello'", "hello"]
```

The point at which no means can coordinate the gathering at all, the hold cluster situation will end up being that of an indistinct hold. The last match is the only one to be displayed in exhibit when a gathering is said to be coordinated on occasions which are more than once.

```
console.log(/bad(ly)?/.exec("bad")); // → ["bad", undefined]
console.log(/(\d)+/.exec("123")); // → ["123", "3"]
```

It is important to note the value of gatherings when it comes to the extraction of portions of a string. In case you do not want to waste time checking if a string has a Date, just erase it and simply create an item that will communicate with it. This can be done by the folding of enclosures over examples of digits and also directly selecting a date from the executive consequence. Note that initially you have to start by going in a different direction which is what is known as the method of inherent used to communicate with time and date in Java.

The JavaScript said to be the class of Date is said to contain a class that is said to be standard for the dates to speak or aim for time.

This is what is called Date. By making use of the item date, you will obtain the current date and time as per now.

```
console.log(new Date()); // → Mon Sep 13 2019 16:19:11 GMT+0100 (CET)
```

It is also possible for you to be the creator of an object within a specified period as well.

```
console.log(new Date(2019, 09, 9)); // → Wed Sep 09 2019 00:00:00
GMT+0100 (CET) console.log(new Date(2009, 11, 9, 12, 59, 59, 999)); // →
Wed Sep 09 2019 12:59:59 GMT+0100 (CET)
```

JavaScript is known to make use of shows whereby numbers of months begin with zero and this makes 11 December but it is worth noting that those of days are known to begin with one. This is said to be very puzzling and even redundant.

Therefore it is important you take caution now that you know the contentions which are four in number and include hours, minutes, seconds, and milliseconds are said to be indicated by zero when they are not available.

When the millisecond quantities are placed away as stamps of time from the year 1970 which is what is known as the UTC zone of time. This is in pursuant to the set of show by "Unix time" which is known to have been designed at that point in time. Use numbers that are negative to indicate periods of time before the year 1970.

The technique fondly known as the getTime is the one used in the restoration of such numbers and is known to be very big as well.

```
console.log(new Date(2013, 11, 19).getTime()); // → 1387407600000
console.log(new Date(1387407600000)); // → Thu Dec 19 2013 00:00:00
GMT+0100 (CET)
```

When you give the constructor of the date a contention that is said to be solitary in nature, the said contention will be used as a tally that is timed to the millisecond.

It is possible for you to obtain the tally that is timed to the millisecond by creating a date article that is similar and asking for getTime for it or by simply being the one to call the Date which is currently what is working.

Of date give techniques include getFullYear ,getMonth ,getDate ,getHours ,getMinutes, and getSeconds to extract portions. It is important to note also getFullYear there's likewise getYear, permitting the user to use the year before 1900 which is not at all possible to be honest.

Placement of parentheses surrounding the components in the expression which picks your interest can at the present moment be a creator of an object date derived from a string.

```
function getDate(string) { let [_, month, day, year] = /(\d{1,2})-(\d{1,2})-
(\d{4})/.exec(string); return new Date(year, month - 1, day); }
console.log(getDate("1-30-2003")); // → Thu Jan 30 2003 00:00:00
GMT+0100 (CET)
```

The utilization and overlooking of the restricted underscore _ is in order to evade the component known to be a full match in the group brought back by the principal.

Others that will gladly remove the date which is not arousing 00-1-3000 are string and words that are limited to getDate.

It is important to note that matches are known to occur anywhere within the string and can start at the character that is said to be subsequent and wind up at the one that is said to be second to last.

8.3 Test ()

When there is a need to input the match there is a need to overcome the string in its entirety and therefore make use of the characters ^ and $.

It is the caret that arranges the start of the string of information. The $ sign of the dollar is indicative of the conclusion. The charged with the mandate to match a string that has one number altogether is /^\d+$/ while /^!/ arranges strings known to begin with a mark to shout while/x^/ are not allowed to make arrangements for any string. Still you are only to require making sure the dates begin with and ends on a limit of words and you can make use of \b which is a marker of sorts.

Limit in words indicates the start or the end of the string and similarly such a position in any string as well which was known to contain a limit in word (as in \w) on one side and a no word character on the other.

```
console.log(/cat/.test("concatenate")); // → true
console.log(/\bcat\b/.test("concatenate")); // → false
```

It is important to take note that marking of the boundary will not be able to be similar to any character in actuality. Its sole purpose is to regulate the expression that is regular and ensure it matches after some conditions are met at a stated point within the pattern.

Examples of decisions indicate the need for knowledge where either a content bit that is small has a number in it in similarity to a number followed by the pig, cows, chicken words or their plurality as well. Therefore, you are able to create articulations that are three in number and be able to put them to trial but there is a better way of doing all of this. The character pipe (|) symbolizes a conclusion after a result from one side and that of the opposite side and therefore you would be right to say that:

```
let animalCount = /\b\d+ (pig|cow|chicken)s?\b/;
console.log(animalCount.test("15 pigs"));

// → true console.log(animalCount.test("15 pigchickens")); // → false
```

You can make good use of brackets in order to limit the example piece applied by the administrator of the pipe and it is possible to have such administrators placed in application arranged with one another in order to explain the conclusion that had a number of choices.

In order to arrange conceptuality, the mechanics needed while using the test and or executive, the articulation that is customary searches for a similar one in the string you have using the tactic of matching the expression initially at the beginning of the string . This will end up two ways with one way of restoring the arranged principal that will be traced or forget to divulge that any match was found at all. In order to properly arrange , an articulation that is standard is treated by the motor in a similar way to a chart of a stream. Below is a chart used to display how animals are domesticated with a past model articulation:

```
"boundary boundary
Group #1
"chicken"
"cow"
"pig"
digit "s"
```

There is a match in the demeanor we have in case we set our eyes on a path leading from the half on the left side of the outline to the side that is the right one. In the string, maintain a situation that is present so that every moment we move inside a crate, we affirm that the string piece after our current place arranges such a case.

Therefore in case we try to arrange the pigs that are three in number from the fourth point, advancing inside the outline of the stream is similar to # Point 4 has a limitation of word examining we are able to proceed to the box that is principal #Also at point 4 there is a number therefore we are able to proceed after the box that follows as well. #Point 5 One paths go back to where we came from in the box that was number 2 while the other path proceeds ahead inside the one that has a character that is solitary in character. Here there is no digit but only space therefore proceed with the other # Point 6 where you are now at which is at the start for the pigs and also on the graph is at route three.

You only see pig and not chicken or bovine therefore it is the right branch to take. #Point 9 following the branch that has three paths in which path one evades the box s while proceeding onwards to the limit which if the last word and the other path arranges. Here there is a character s without a limit to word therefore there is an experience of the box s.

At the ending point 10 which is the finishing point is where we are at and are only able to arrange limited words.

At the end of a string there is a consideration of a limit in word. The string ends to put into consideration the limit of word in order to have a look at box that is at the end and able to arrange well the string. Tracking back the articulation that is Ordinary /\b([01]+b|[\da-f]+h|\d+)\b/ arranges a number that is double followed by a muscle of the stomach, a number that is a hexadecimal which has a 16 base together with the letters a to f indicative of the numbers 10-15 and is followed by a h or by a decimal number that is normally lacking the charter to add.

An example of a chart for comparison:

word boundary
group #1
One of: "o" "1"
"b"
One of: digit -" a" "f"
"h"
digit
word boundary

During the coordination of the articulation, it is possible that the branch at the top is breached even when the info lacked a number that was paired. During coordination of the 103 string as a sample, there is more indication of clarity at the point of 3 which had been placed in the branch they should not have been in. The articulation if matched by the string and in the branch we are currently in.

The one matching will track back. Upon entrance to a branch, it remembers its current position (position in which at the string start, just past the limit that is primary chart enclosed) hoping it will come back and be able to try another branch in case the one at hand malfunctions. The 103 string after witnessing the number 3 is charged with the mandate to start trying the branch with numbers that are hexadecimal but fails too because of lack of h in front of the number. Therefore it tries the branch number decimal. It is a perfect fit and with all things considered a match is registered and the one matching ends the task after finding the match that is full.

There is an indication that branches that are different can be able to make arrangements to a string but only the initial (asked for by the place the branches are witnessed in the articulation that is said to be normal) to be used. Tracking back also happens to redundancy administrators similar to + and *. In the event that you coordinate/^.*x/against "abcxe", the .* portion at first will try to remove the string in its entirety. Here the motor will grasp the concept that it requires a x in order to arrange the example. Because of lack of an x after the conclusion of the string, the one administering the string star will try to arrange by removing a character. Be that as it may,the one matching will not be able to identify the x following abcx too and will therefore go back again and will coordinate the administrator that is star to a simple abc.

At the momentit locates a x at the moment it is required and gives feedback to a match that is positive from the point of 0-4. It is possible to create articulations that can be said to be customary and are able to do a very wide range of tracking backwards. This occurs when a sample is able to arrange a contribution in a large number in a variety of paths. An example in case we are confused in any way, shape or form as we are creating an articulation that is said to be paired in number, we can at the same time build one the same as

$$/([01]+)+b/.$$

"b"
Group #1
One of:
"1"
"0"

In the event that that attempts to coordinate arrangements that are seen to be very long in terms of ones and zeros lacking a character b following, the one matching will get to feels the circle which is inside to the point where it lacks numbers. At that point it sees there is nob, so it will backtrack one position, experience the external circle once, and after that surrender once more, attempting to backtrack out of the inward circle yet again. It will keep on difficult each conceivable course through these two circles meaning the measure of copies of work following every character that is extra.

Even a few numbers of characters like a dozen, the match has gotten gets for all intents and purposes forever.hing like/([01]+)+b/.

8.4 Replace ()

The string method of replacing is known to contain digits that can be utilized a string portion with another string portion.

```
console.log("papa".replace("p", "m")); // → mapa
```

The argument at the start is allowed to be an expression that is regular meaning the initial expression that is regular is replaceable. With the addition of the option g (worldwide) to the expression which is regular, there is therefore replacement of all string that match, not the initial one only.

```
console.log("Borobudur".replace(/[ou]/, "a")); // → Barobudur
console.log("Borobudur".replace(/[ou]/g, "a")); // → Barabadar
```

It would have been reasonable if the decision between supplanting one match or all matches was made through an extra contention to supplant or by giving an alternate technique, supplant All.

Be that as it may, for some awful reason, the decision depends on a property of the customary articulation. The genuine intensity of utilizing normal articulations with supplant originates from the insignificant truth that you can allude to coordinated gatherings in the string of substitution. A sample of this is when you indicate you have a string that is major and has some people's names with every name in only one line following the pattern of the second name, the first name. When there is a need to switch the names and get rid of the comma to remain with last name first name, the code below can be of use:

```
console.log( "Liskov, Barbara\nMcCarthy, John\nWadler, Philip"
.replace(/(\w+), (\w+)/g, "$2 $1")); // → Barbara Liskov // John McCarthy
// Philip Wadler
```

The $1 and $2 in the substitution string allude to the parenthesized bunches in the example. $1 is supplanted by the content that coordinated against the principal gathering, $2 continuously, etc, up to $9. The entire match can be alluded to with $&. It is really conceivable to pass a capacity—as opposed to a string—as the subsequent contention to supplant.

For every substitution, the capacity will be called with the coordinated gatherings as contentions and its arrival worth is attached to the string that is new. A model for this is below:

```
let s = "the cia and fbi"; console.log(s.replace(/\b(fbi|cia)\b/g, str =>
str.toUpperCase())); // → the CIA and FBI
```

An even more awesome sample is below:

```
let stock = "1 lemon, 2 cabbages, and 101 eggs"; function minusOne(match,
amount, unit) { amount = Number(amount) - 1; if (amount == 1) { // only
one left, remove the 's' unit = unit.slice(0, unit.length - 1); } else if (amount
== 0) { amount = "no"; } return amount + " " + unit; }
console.log(stock.replace(/(\d+) (\w+)/g, minusOne)); // → no lemon, 1
cabbage, and 100 eggs
```

A string is obtained then learns a number's events in full which were sought by the word which utilized both alphabets and numbers and gave back the string in which every event has to be decremeted by each one. (\d+) is a bunch used to end the contention measure the capacity uses while the bunch (\w+) is attached to the unit.

The capacity makes changes of the sum which results in a digit and this always works because it is guided by (\d+) which does not make many changes when there is only a zero or one left.

8.5 The Method of searching

Using articulation that is ordinary, it is impossible to call the strategy of indexOf. Anyway there is another technique, search that expects a standard articulation. Smilar to indexOf, it is expected to deliver back the file that is dominant which contained the articulation or a negative one in the off chance it was missing.

```
console.log(" word".search(/\S/));
// → 2 console.log(" ".search(/\S/)); // → -1
```

The downside is the lack of a path to display the start of the match at a specified point because this would be a plus.

8.6 Pattern Method

You presently realize how to coordinate a solitary digit. Consider the possibility that you needed to coordinate an entire number an arrangement of at least one digit. When you put an or more sign (+) subsequent to something in a standard articulation, it shows that the component could be rehashed more than one time and in this way,/\d+/matches at least one digit characters.

```
console.log(/'\d+'/.test("'123'")); // → true console.log(/'\d+'/.test("''")); // → false
console.log(/'\d*'/.test("'123'")); // → true console.log(/'\d*'/.test("''")); // → true
```

The similarity is observed in significance for the star (*) yet furthermore empowers the guide to coordinate on numerous occasions.

Anything which has the star in front of it will not be able to defend any model from being organized because all it will be able to do is compare zero cases whenever it is able to locate substance that is sensible in order for it to be arranged.

Leading using a mark of questioning on the other hand makes a bit of a model optional, which means it could happen on numerous occasions or once only. The following model utilizes the character u by permitting it to appear plus the model appears too when it is not there.

```
let neighbor = /neighbou?r/; console.log(neighbor.test("neighbour")); // →
true console.log(neighbor.test("neighbor")); // → true
```

Braces are used particularly to signal when a specific pattern is displayed a number of times. Placing {4} in front of a specific element after an element, for instance, requires it to occur exactly four times. There is also a possibility for a range to be specified an example is {2,4} which is indicative of the element being able to appear more than once but not exceeding four times. Another example to observe is one of the time patterns and date as well displayed by its capacity to allow more than one number but not exceeding two hours, or days or months as well. This is known to be easy to understand.

```
let dateTime = /\d{1,2}-\d{1,2}-\d{4} \d{1,2}:\d{2}/;
console.log(dateTime.test("1-30-2003 8:45")); // → true
```

8.7 String Patterns

String esteems have a supplant strategy that could be utilized to supplant portions with another of that particular string.

```
console.log("papa".replace("p", "m")); // → mapa
```

The main contention can likewise be an ordinary articulation, where case the principal match of the customary articulation is supplanted. The exact moment when the alternative g (global) is combined with the articulation that is said to be customary, every single match is supplanted in the string.

```
console.log("Borobudur".replace(/[ou]/, "a")); // → Barobudur
console.log("Borobudur".replace(/[ou]/g, "a")); // → Barabadour
```

8.8 Summary

Ordinary articulations are objects that speak to designs in strings and utilize their own language to express these examples.

Strings are said to contain a strategy for matching in order to group them against articulation that is said to be customary and a technique which is a quest used for scanning and rewinding them to the initial match which was a situation. Their supplant technique could supplant matches of an example with a substitution string or a capacity.

They can have choices, which are composed after the end slice. The choice presents the match defense heartless. The g choice makes the articulation worldwide, which, in addition to other things, causes the supplant strategy to supplant all occurrences rather than simply the first.

The y alternative makes it clingy, which implies that it won't look forward and skip some portion of the string when searching for a match.

The u choice turns on Unicode mode, which fixes various issues around the treatment of characters that take up two code units.

Ordinary articulations are a sharp device with an unbalanced handle. They are capable of streamlining a few undertakings massively yet can rapidly end up unmanageable when applied to complex issues. Part of this portion is to actively make a discovery of their existence and use while refuting the urge of using shortcuts to achieve the same results while they can perfectly be able to sound in them. Shortcuts are not always the best option as they might end up accumulating errors that will only demand the programmer to start all over again.

Chapter 9: HTML5 APIS

HTML5 is a term that of late has come to be used to describe the latest HTML version specifications as well as all the web application technologies currently being developed side by side with HTML. These new technologies are known as Open Web Platform.

The various APIs include:

I.   Geolocation.

Geolocation is an API that is known to allow JavaScript programs to inquire from the browser being used the real-time location of the specific user. These applications that know locations can be used to display maps, specified directions as well as certain information involving matters that relate to where the specific user is currently located. This application has come with its specific security concerns in terms of revealing such sensitive information about the user. This is why the browser always asks for permission before allowing the JavaScript program to display the location of the user.

Browsers have known to support the Geolocation APIs define **navigator.geolocation** which is a property that is in reference to three specified methods. These methods include:

- navigator.geolocation.getcurrentPosition().

This is described as the one that requests the user's current location.

- navigator.geolocation.watchPosition().

This is described as the one that requests the current position and still continues to monitor the specified position then follows this by invoking the required call back when the location of the user changes.

- navigation.geolocation.clearWatch()

This is the one described as the one to halt watch of the user's location. It is described as the method that should have the number which will be returned by the specific Watchposition().

Every device that is known to use GPS (Global Position Systems) is said to be able to access very precise information from the specific GPS unit. It is important to note that information on location originates mostly from the web. When a browser is enabled to give your IP address to a website, it is very easy then to locate the specific city you are in.

A more precise location can be provided to the browser by it requesting the system for operation for a list of close by networks that are said to be wireless plus providing their specific strength of a particular signal. With the use of a sophisticated algorithm, it is easy to narrow down your exact location.

Geolocation APIs are heavily dependent on the exchange of information by use of networks or in some cases satellites.

An example of location requests is:

```
navigator.geolocation.getCurrentPosition(function(pos) {
    var latitude=pos.coords.latitude
    var longitude=pos.coords.longitude;

    alert("yourposition: "+latitude+" +longitude);
});
```

II.   History Management

Web programs are empowered with the capacities to be able to keep a record of what archives have been shown in a window. This is made possible by the availability of different caches installed in the programs that empower the client to have access to a particular or a chain of records that they need at any particular moment. This is back when the browsing records had been rendered inactive as soon as a client had exited from the browser. In order for the client to have ready access to the history records then, they had to be accessed exclusively on the servers that had been used to host the sites or pages that the client had visited previously in the past.

Today a client can be able to show new states applications without the stacking of new records. While utilizing HTML5, there are two systems that are useful in the execution of history recovery when required by the client at any particular time.

The less difficult history can be the boarding procedure: This method is the one which includes the location of the pages that the client viewed together with the hash and what is known as the hash change occasion.

In numerous programs the location.hash setting prompts the URL showed naturally refreshing prompting a section in the program history. It is in the wake of setting it that a client actually has the options to view and utilize the history that they browsed in a forward and back motion to explore all the reports.

In history management, there are a number of ways to use this technique. For instance, it is simpler still to make use of the technique which is said to involve the location.hash the event which is said to also be the hash change as well. The same technique can also be described as having to be able to be put to use on a larger location in the world today and it is important to note that there are those browsers that were already making use of it even prior to the period when HTML5 made it standard. In many browsers it is said to be set in such a way that the URL properties are the ones to be updated where the bar is located and is also responsible for the addition of an entry as well in the in the ID which was used in the olden days of any documentation which can be scrolled as well. The property referred to as hash is the one charged with the mandate to get the ID of the element and have it viewed by any string that needs to.

By getting a string to be what you have used to encode the application that you were making use of then it is that exact string that can be utilized also as an identifier of the string as well.

How the property location.hash is to be set will also in turn enable the one using it to have the ability to make use of the buttons for back and forth which is how they will travel in between the states of the various documents available.

In order for this to function correctly, the application you made use of must should be enabled with the ability to detect the state changes in order for it to be able to read and communicate the identifier of fragments which is in storage and also be able to make updates to itself in whichever manner is needed at the present time. HTML5 is enabled with the ability of its browser to be able to shoot forth an event of hashchange which is directed to one which will handle it in terms of a function which is what will be summoned any time there is a need for the identifier of fragment to navigate the history which is now in storage.

The moment the function of the one handling it is summoned, the summon must proceed beyond the value of the location.hash and be able to display once more the information that is contained in the state application as well.

There is also a more difficult and complex method that is defined by HTML5 for the management of history which will involve the method of push state history and also the event which is said to be post state as well. It is the point where an app of web goes into a new state that the push state of history is summoned to include that specified state to the history of the browser as well. it is worth noting that any object that can be turned into a form of a string can also be changeable and can work well.

III.   Messaging that is cross-origin

There is total isolation that is witnessed in plain sight in the browser of windows as well as in some tabs. In some instances whenever a script is able to display windows that are completely new or is able to make use of frames which were previously nested, the numerous numbers of frames and windows will be able to have a form interaction with one another and also to make some form of a manipulation with the documents of one another as well.

There are also some instances to take note of when a script may be called upon to make reference to yet another object of a window but due to the information on the said window having originated from another place of origin it will not be able to fully view the origin of that previous document too. It is also important to note that this browser will not permit the script to be able to read the properties or be involved in any methods of invoking with tat window as well. The method of messaging in a manner which can cross message will make the event of the message be viewed as one that can be made use of whenever there is a need for the inclusion of the modular from a site which is from a different area but still inside of your page of the web. With the gadget being of a very simple nature and also being able to be contained within itself, there is a way in which you can be able to isolate it too. With a more complex one which is the one charged with the mandate to define the API and it is the duty of your web page to be able to manage it or be able to also communicate with it as well.

The messaging the is of a cross nature is able to give us an alternative in which the writer of the gadget can be able to pack it within a file which is from the HTML which will be the one to be able to hear the events of messages and be the one to deploy the same messages to the function of JavaScript which can be said to be the most appropriate one too. This will mean the webpage which will have the gadget as well will be able to communicate with it by deploying messages with the postmessage command. JavaScript is said to also have browsers that have only one thread and wont at any time be able to run events that are more than one at a similar time and also there will be no timer triggering while a handler of events is also running at the very same time.

Conclusion

We've made considerable progress, from hi world to a content that acknowledges client info and changes the whole page. This has been a great deal of JavaScript over a short number of pages, so in the event that you didn't get each and every definition or punch each piece of code into your support, don't perspire it.

As guaranteed, we've just barely scarcely start to expose every one of the things JavaScript can do and JavaScript is continually developing like some other web standard. We can't know everything and well never need to as the world of programing changes every single day to suit the needs and requirements that the people are in need of. JavaScript is a wide language that individuals often specialize in different sections that are not similar to others making it a very diverse language but with the same aim of manipulating computers.

For instance the presentation of hub has changed the game. Hub is a decent, little framework that gives us a chance to run JavaScript in a no program setting.

It was initially intended for system errands to assume the job of a hub in a system. Be that as it may, it fits a wide range of errands that are said to be scripted and in JavaScript composition is one you have to be grateful for because of the admiration of assignments that are mechanized.

NPM gives bundles to all that you can consider (and many things you'd most likely never consider), and it enables you to bring and introduce those bundles with the npm program. Hub goes hand in hand with a variety of modules that are implicit and some of them are of the module fs which function with the framework of record together with the module of HTTP servers plus making demands of HTTP as well. In the Node, all the information together with the yield is executed in a manner that is not concurrent with the only exception being when without doubt you make use of a variation which is said to be synchronized in capacity with an example being readFileSync. It is important to note that during the call of these capacities that are said to be offbeat, you will be required to give capacities that are said to be callback.

Here is where Node will summon each with esteem which is blunder (if accessible) when prepared to get an outcome.

Last but not least, JavaScript is a constructive and dangerous language as well. Programmers can use the language to code and make destructive commands that destroy and affects the swift running of computers. A good example of that could be the creation of malware software that destroys huge companies exposing all their data to the public. Other destructive examples that's JavaScript programming could be harmful is the rise of cyberbullying and hacking that happens to data storage companies by the hackers and they demand ransoms in order not to expose the data that could possibly do lots of harm to the company.

The knowledge of JavaScript is by far very important to acquire as is serves as the backbone of computer sophistication which can prove to be very efficient and important especially in the growing world of science and technology.

www.ingramcontent.com/pod-product-compliance
Lightning Source LLC
Chambersburg PA
CBHW071106050326
40690CB00008B/1137